THE
MYSTICISM
OF THE
PRESENT
MOMENT

EMBODIED SPIRITUALITY

José Tolentino Mendonça

Paulist Press
New York / Mahwah, NJ

The Scripture quotations contained herein are from the New Revised Standard Version: Catholic Edition, Copyright © 1989 and 1993, by the Division of Christian Education of the National Council of the Churches of Christ in the United States of America. Used by permission. All rights reserved.

Cover image by agsandrew/iStock.com
Cover design by Sharyn Banks
Book design by Lynn Else

First published as *A Mística do Instante* © 2014, Instituto Missionário Filhas de São Paulo—Paulinas Editora
Rua Francisco Salgado Zenha, *A Mística do Instante* 11, 2685-332 Prior Velho, Portugal, www.paulinas.pt

English translation copyright © 2021 by Paulist Press

All rights reserved. No part of this publication may be reproduced, stored in a retrieval system, or transmitted in any form or by any means, electronic, mechanical, photocopying, recording, scanning, or otherwise, without either the prior written permission of the Publisher, or authorization through payment of the appropriate per-copy fee to the Copyright Clearance Center, Inc., www.copyright.com. Requests to the Publisher for permission should be addressed to the Permissions Department, Paulist Press, permissions@paulistpress.com.

Library of Congress Cataloging-in-Publication Data
Names: Mendonça, José Tolentino, author.
Title: The mysticism of the present moment : embodied spirituality / José Tolentino Mendonça.
Other titles: Mistica do Instante. English
Description: New York / Mahwah, NJ : Paulist Press, 2021. | "First published as A Mistica do Instante. 2014, Instituto Missionário Filhas de São Paul—Paulinas Editora. Rua Francisco Salgado Zenha, A Mistica do Instante 11, 2685–332 Prior Velho, Portugal." | Includes bibliographical references. | Summary: "Based on biblical revelation and contributions from anthropology, José Tolentino Mendonça offers a spirituality of the present moment that involves the senses and the body in the expression of faith. It shows how our body, through the senses, opens us to the presence of God in the moment"— Provided by publisher.
Identifiers: LCCN 2020037708 (print) | LCCN 2020037709 (ebook) | ISBN 9780809155323 (paperback) | ISBN 9781587689284 (ebook)
Subjects: LCSH: Spirituality—Catholic Church. | Senses and sensation—Religious aspects—Catholic Church. | Human body—Religious aspects—Catholic Church. | God (Christianity)—Knowableness.
Classification: LCC BX2350.65 .M4513 2021 (print) | LCC BX2350.65 (ebook)| DDC 248—dc23
LC record available at https://lccn.loc.gov/2020037708
LC ebook record available at https://lccn.loc.gov/2020037709

ISBN 978-0-8091-5532-3 (paperback)
ISBN 978-1-58768-928-4 (e-book)

Published by Paulist Press
997 Macarthur Boulevard
Mahwah, New Jersey 07430
www.paulistpress.com

Printed and bound in the
United States of America

A mystic is someone who cannot stop walking.

—Michel de Certeau, *The Mystic Fable*

CONTENTS

FOREWORD

Our time is marked by incredible connectivity and access to vast amounts of information, which has shifted our time and attention from the world before us to the world behind the screen and across the web. Situated in our own digital worlds, we are challenged by a kind of "contemporary Gnosticism," as Pope Francis has put it, that prioritizes our thoughts and ideas, opinions and critiques, to the detriment of the physical, embodied, and incarnational wholeness for which God made us and into which God entered personally as the Incarnate Word. In recent years, Pope Francis has cautioned us to avoid becoming like those who "think of the intellect as separate from the flesh, and thus become incapable of touching Christ's suffering flesh in others, locked up as they are in an encyclopedia of abstractions" (*Gaudete et Exsultate* 37). If our faith is one centered on the core belief that God became flesh (*sarx* in Greek), then a Christian spirituality for our time must begin and end with this important affirmation of our embodiment. And this is exactly what Cardinal José Tolentino Mendonça offers readers in this timely and moving book.

Cardinal Mendonça's writing weaves together a beautiful tapestry of poetry, Scripture, art, philosophy, and theology that speaks to the heart of our contemporary circumstances. His vision of spiritual life aligns well with that of Pope Francis's because they both share a commitment to the centrality of Christ's incarnation as the starting point of our faith. From the outset, Cardinal Mendonça draws from the deep well of the Christian tradition to provide readers with a "unified vision of the human person," one that is not a disembodied intellect or collection of opinions, but an integrated whole that God intended from the first moment of creation. Celebrating the gift of our corporeality, Cardinal Mendonça writes poetically and profoundly that "our body that we are is a divine grammar," for God not only designed this creaturely reality of which we are an integrated part, but God also freely chose to communicate God's self most fully to us precisely *within and as part of creation* in Jesus Christ.

Although Cardinal Mendonça is not yet well known among North American English speakers, this beautiful book reflects well his pastoral and spiritual vision of Christian discipleship to a broad audience. In defining mysticism, he follows in the footsteps of giants like Jesuit Fr. Karl Rahner, one of the leading Catholic theologians of the twentieth century, who famously stated, "The Christian of the future will be a mystic, or he [or she] will not exist at all." Spirituality and mysticism are not limited experiences for the Christian elite or for canonized saints alone, but essential to the experience of full human flourishing. Cardinal Mendonça is also drawn to a powerful yet deceptively minimal description of mysticism offered by the late philosopher Michel de Certeau: "A mystic is someone 'who cannot stop walking.'" In this short sentence, we hear yet another echo of Pope Francis's spiritual outlook and love of the image of walking for Christian life. It is dynamic, ongoing, inclusive, experiential, and pilgrimage focused. Such a view of the profound encounter with the divine in our everyday lives is a refreshing reminder that God is found in the mundane and ordinary, along the roadside or in our workplace or in the midst of our busy family lives, and not merely in the rarefied realm of monasteries and hermitages.

The greatest contribution of this volume is Cardinal Mendonça's reintroduction of the bodily senses into the Christian spiritual life. For centuries, the role of the senses, physical and spiritual, had occupied a place of significance in the Christian spiritual tradition. But in the wake of the Western Enlightenment exaltation of reason beyond anything physical, material, corporeal, empirical, or sensual, this sense of embodied spirituality in the Christian experience has been diminished. Today's digital age only exacerbates the modern person's incredulity about the finite and physical world as the privileged location of God's revelation and presence. And yet, Cardinal Mendonça beautifully draws from wisdom ancient and modern to correct this misperception. He reminds us that touch, taste, smell, hearing, and sight are the means through which we experience God's grace in the everyday experience of human life. Each of these senses provides the very condition of the possibility for divine encounter, provided, of course, we learn to attune these senses for this purpose. One's physical hearing may be excellent, but without the spiritual practice of attunement, we might never recognize God's presence in the "sheer silence" as did the prophet Elijah (1 Kgs 19:12). One's sight might be 20/20, but without training our gaze on the world around us to see anew, we might regularly miss the Creator's love proclaimed all around us by the rest of creation.

The full actualization of our embodied spirituality is not an end in itself, but a means toward a more profound reality for which each of God's creatures was made: *relationship*. This is something Cardinal Mendonça makes clear at the end of his inspired reflections. He explains, "The key to understanding mysticism, and in particular a mysticism of the present moment, is the word *relationship*." Engaging our physical and spiritual senses draws us out of our tendency toward solipsism, self-centeredness, and isolation, and outward toward connection with God, others, and all creation. For this we were made, but so much of our modern world is designed to dull and distract us, to lull us into an unwitting slumber. This book is a loving wake-up call, an invitation to see ourselves and the world in a new light, to hear the quiet voice of God always present, to feel the grace around us, to smell the beautiful scent of sanctity that is creation, and to taste the life that God has promised us to have—and to have abundantly (John 10:10).

Cardinal Mendonça is a scripture scholar by training and a poet by vocation, which provide the unique skill set seen on display in each sentence of this extraordinary book. At one glance, the contents seem simple and direct, but upon further reflection, the richness of wisdom contained within these pages begins to flood the heart and mind of each reader. It is a gift to the English-speaking world to have access to this treasure, and it is my hope that this book might serve as a gateway through which many more Christians and other people of goodwill can deepen their spiritual lives through the writings of Cardinal Mendonça.

Daniel P. Horan, OFM
Duns Scotus Professor of Spirituality
Catholic Theological Union, Chicago
Feast of All Saints 2020

PART ONE

A SPIRITUALITY FOR OUR TIME

Spirituality. Another word for it might be *interiority*, and interiority is closely related to the idea of *mysticism*. "Close the door of your senses and seek God in the depths of yourself," proposed one of the advocates of eighteenth-century pietism. This statement is a good example of what we might call a "mysticism of the soul." It's the idea that the path that leads us to God is fundamentally an interior one, one that requires us to relativize or even to renounce our bodily senses. To reach the divine, it tells us, the soul needs to dive into itself. The divine is beyond the faculties of the body and its contingencies; we can only find it through the radar of strict interiority. The divine is mystery. Approaching it requires detaching ourselves from the everyday world and looking within ourselves where the divine presence dwells.

In a work that greatly influenced the Christian imagination, with the emblematic title *On True Religion*, St. Augustine wrote, "Do not go outside yourself, but return to within yourself; truth dwells in the inner person."[1] Much of Christian mysticism, from the oldest to the most contemporary, has been a development of this basic idea.

1

It's a reminder of the importance of understanding this precious heritage in the light of a more complete anthropology. The great St. John of the Cross, for example, in the second half of the sixteenth century, explained that the more the soul empties of its natural operations, the more surely it advances. For him, making progress in the spiritual life involves experiencing the "night of the senses," seeking "the spiritual and the interior" while struggling against "the imperfect spirit of the sensual and the exterior."

This model of Christian mysticism persisted closer to our own day. There is a plaque in the heart of downtown Louisville, Kentucky, that marks the location of the "second conversion" of the Trappist monk Thomas Merton, which took place there in 1958. By then, Merton was already a world-famous spiritual author. The book that had made him famous, ten years prior, was his autobiography, *The Seven Storey Mountain*. It had inspired millions of readers to delve deeper into contemplative prayer—and the paradigm of the spiritual life as a flight from the world is present throughout it. A decade later, walking through the streets of Louisville, amid the frenzy of the crowd in its busy commercial district, Merton received the insight that in the end, there was no difference or separation between himself and all the people who made up this anonymous and thirsty crowd. He understood, simply and vibrantly, what it was to be a member of the human family, of which the Son of God chose to be a part. This realization corrected the error of Merton's previous period and opened a new stage of his spirituality. Merton perceived that mysticism was inseparable from daily living, uniting and integrating all aspects of life.

MORE SPIRITUALITY IN OUR BODIES

The excessive internalization of spiritual experience, on one hand, and the distancing of the body and of the world, on the other, still largely characterize spirituality as it is practiced today. What is spiritual is considered superior to what we experience through the senses. We understand the spiritual as a complex, precious, and profound reality, while we perceive the senses as superficial and a bit frivolous. It is symptomatic to note that the way of life of consecrated religious men or women is often understood to be somehow *disembodied*—they voluntarily take up a position of otherness in relation to the world, from which they are distant or even foreign. In what we might call a "mysticism of the soul," the divine Spirit is radically separated from the present moment and from the sad experience of creatures living in time.

The narrative realism of the Bible, however, offers a potent remedy for this thinking, right from the start. In fact, the common dissociations of the soul from the body, of the interior from the exterior, of religious practice from daily life, are absent from the core of biblical revelation. At the center of that revelation is life, the life that God loves because, as Jesus teaches, God "is God not of the dead, but of the living" (Matt 22:32). Likewise, it includes no aversion to the body. This is what we read in Genesis:

> These are the generations of the heavens and the earth when they were created.
>
> In the day that the LORD God made the earth and the heavens, when no plant of the field was yet in the earth and no herb of the field had yet sprung up—for the LORD God had not caused it to rain upon the earth, and there was no one to till the ground; but a stream would rise from the earth, and water the whole face of the ground—then the LORD God formed man from the dust of the ground, and breathed into his nostrils the breath of life; and the man became a living being. (Gen 2:4–7)

What is this "breath of life"? It is nothing less than God's own breath—God's Spirit who acts in every living being, experienced as the very source of existence and manifested through the senses and the vital functions of the human person. In the act of creation (i.e., from the beginning of the beginnings), a beautiful and irrevocable covenant was established between divine Spirit and earthly life. If that's the case, then where can we experience the Spirit of God, if not in the depths of our living flesh? Where will we encounter God's own breath, if not in the very "dust" into which God breathed? How can we open ourselves to perceive God's presence, if not through our senses?

The Bible's vision, then, is markedly different from "spiritual-ist" ways of thinking. The Bible offers a unified vision of the human person. There the body is never perceived as the outer shell of a spiritual principle, nor as a prison of the soul, as did Platonism and so many of the philosophies that followed it. In God's creation, the body is in the image and likeness of God (see Gen 1:27). As the sacramental theologian Louis-Marie Chauvet wrote, "The most 'spiritual' happens through the most 'corporeal.'"[2] Given all of this, we might therefore paraphrase Nietzsche's well-known comment, "There is more reason in your body than in your best wisdom,"[3] to say, "There is more spiri-tuality in our bodies than in our best theology."

THE BODY IS GOD'S MOTHER TONGUE

Anchored in the divine seed of which we are not only contain-ers, but which is constitutive of our being, we are called to embrace the prodigious excess that is *life* in a creative way and with all our senses. The experience of life is an immense laboratory in which we can—with our attention, our sensitivity, and our capacity for wonder—recognize in every moment the reflection of the extraordi-nary presence of God. We need to take a new look at *the body that we are* and at our existence, seeing them as prophecies of unconditional love: "For God so loved the world that he gave his only Son, so that everyone who believes in him may not perish but may have eternal life" (John 3:16).

Our body that we are is a divine grammar. It is through this body (and not only through our mind) that we learn. The French philosopher Maurice Merleau-Ponty—known as the philosopher of the body and embodiment—rightly notes that our connection with our mother tongue begins through our bodies, long before we learn to talk. The sound of words inhabits us; they become buried very early in the hidden memory of our body. They are inscribed in our sleep and tattooed on our skin. The language of God is no different. The psalms offer this wonderful image:

> My frame was not hidden from you,
> when I was being made in secret,
>   intricately woven in the depths of the earth.
> Your eyes beheld my unformed substance.
>   (Ps 139:15–16)

This metaphor shows us that our body is itself a mother tongue—it is the mother tongue of God. And so the *mysticism of the senses, or of the present moment*, that we are going to consider here (as an alternative to a "mysticism of the soul") is simply a spirituality that understands *the senses as a path and a doorway to encountering God*.

"This radical mystery [of God's revelation]," wrote the theologian Karl Rahner, "is nearness and not distance, self-surrendering love and not judgement."[4] We can find God in all that we experience. It's not about retreating into our inner world and ignoring everything else. The challenge is to be present to ourselves and to experience with all our senses the reality of what comes to us and of the One who comes to us. The challenge is to throw ourselves into the arms of life—without fleeing it and without idealizing it, the arms of life as it truly is—and to hear there the beat of God's heart.

I think here of the spiritual journal of Etty Hillesum, an incomparable work written in a Nazi concentration camp. In the darkest hours of contemporary history and without any expectation of anyone ever reading her words, Hillesum confided,

> I thought, Is it not strange? It is wartime. There are concentration camps. Small barbarity mounts upon small barbarity....I know the persecution and oppression and despotism and the impotent fury and the terrible sadism. I know it all and continue to confront every shred of reality that thrusts itself upon me. And yet—at unguarded moments, when left to myself, I suddenly lie against the naked breast of life, and her arms round me are so gentle and protective, and my own heartbeat is difficult to describe; so slow and so regular and so soft, almost muffled, but so constant, as if it would never stop.[5]

AN EXHAUSTED SOCIETY

Each era has its own pathologies. They hint at hidden pain, produce behaviors and compulsions, and reveal vulnerabilities that we prefer not to see. The great threat of past centuries was bacterial and viral, and the invention of antibiotics and vaccines has helped bring these health problems under control, even if many remain. The philosopher Byung Chul Han, who has become increasingly well regarded in recent years, tells us that the significant pathologies of the beginning of the twenty-first century are basically neural-emotional in nature. The dark sun of depression, personality disorders, attention deficits, a hyper-activism that leaves us feeling emptied out, like a scorched earth—these characterize the landscape of our time. These sicknesses are not infectious; they stem from the fragility of existence, the fragmentation of identity, the inability to integrate or understand the things we have experienced.

The truth is that our Western societies are facing a silent paradigm shift: *excess*—of emotions, information, expectations, and demands—that damages the integrity of the person and creates a state of fatigue from which it is increasingly difficult to emerge. We risk being trapped permanently in this fatigue, which the Portuguese poet Fernando Pessoa described prophetically:

> I am tired, that is clear,
> Because, at certain stage, people have to be tired.
> Of what I am tired, I don't know:
> It would not serve me at all to know
> Since the tiredness stays just the same.[6]

FIGHTING THE ATROPHY OF THE SENSES

Accende lumen sensus ("Illuminate the senses"), said an ancient liturgical invocation, leaving no doubt about the necessity of the participation of the bodily senses in the experience of faith. *Our body's senses open us to the presence of God in the moment we're living.*

If we are healthy, we have five senses at our disposal (touch, taste, smell, sight, and hearing), but the truth is that we do not develop the use of each sense as fully as we could or, at least, we don't develop them all to an equal degree. We can receive and transmit extremely diverse kinds of information through the senses, which our brain interprets and responds to. However, we lack an education of the senses by which we would learn to use them effectively, to cultivate them, to purify them.

"I don't know what I feel or what I want to feel. I don't know what I think or what I am," wrote Fernando Pessoa.[7] And elsewhere: "I felt too much to go on feeling any further."[8] Indeed, the excess of sensory stimulation into which we are plunged produces the opposite effect: it does not increase our capacity to feel but afflicts it with an irreparable atrophy. "Oh! if at least I could feel!"—this is the expression of contemporary despair that arises after having experienced everything. This numbing of the senses, exacerbated by a cynicism that induces a retreat from life, is an instrument of annihilation: "The skin has taught me nothing," lamented the poet René Crevel in *My Body and I.*[9] This is where the mysticism of the senses can play a crucial role, because through it, as Michel de Certeau explains, "the body is informed." *The skin teaches us.*

There are many circumstances of life, however, that lead us to pathologies of the senses and push us into a kind of asthenia. Let's briefly consider four such experiences: a rejection of suffering, an inability to mourn, an overdependence on routine, and an excess of communication.

SUFFOCATED BY PAIN

We live in a society increasingly dominated by the myth of control. The basic premise, elevated now to the status of a dogma, is that the secret of a fulfilled life lies in our ability to control it 100 percent. We ignore the fact that such a mentality is contrary to reality, and so we are unprepared to handle anything unexpected—especially suffering.

As a result, when we experience pain, it comes upon us like a storm that arises out of nowhere, shocking and inexplicable. We become transfixed by it, and our senses become like shutters that we close up tight, perhaps unconsciously. We close our eyes against light or color, smells bother us, we ignore pleasure, we avoid hearing the melody around us. We are unable to pay attention to anything else around us. "Pain suffocates, it leaves no air. Pain needs space," writes the French novelist Marguerite Duras in her book *La Douleur* (Pain) (Collins, 1986).

As we journey through suffering, our helplessness in the face of it seems, mysteriously, to trap all our resources. We come to doubt that we can live fully, or even partly, the adventure of our lives in this imperfect body of ours. We need resources that help us live with renewed courage and to understand the incapacity caused by pain.

REFUSING TO BE CONSOLED

Virginia Woolf opens her novel *The Waves* in this way: "Gradually as the sky whitened, a dark line lay on the horizon dividing the sea from the sky and the grey cloth became barred with thick strokes moving, one after another, beneath the surface, following each other, pursuing each other, perpetually."[10] Her words evoke very well the experience of mourning.

Loss is also one of those secrets of the body that we find increasingly difficult to face. Death has become taboo. Talking about it publicly is considered as rude and embarrassing as uttering an obscenity. We hide it by all means possible. Then when someone we love is dying, we find ourselves frightened and lonely. We enter a sort of suspended state, a retreat from life, an eclipse of relationships, not only with the outside, but also with our own body.

We need guides who can help us understand death and what it means to our humanity. We first need to mourn our inability to be comforted. What an extraordinary passage we find in the Gospel of Matthew, which the evangelist quotes from the Old Testament, concerning the death of the Holy Innocents:

> A voice was heard in Ramah,
>   wailing and loud lamentation,
> Rachel weeping for her children;
>   she refused to be consoled, because they are no more.
>   (Matt 2:18; cf. Jer 31:15)

We need to weep and to be consoled, little by little, and then gradually integrate absence into a new understanding of this mystery of the presence of others in our life.

THE PRISON OF ROUTINE

Routine emerges when we try to maintain regular rhythms in our daily lives, an effort that is, in itself, positive. Life would be impossible if everything were unplanned and random. Routines are healthy. By structuring our lives with predictable situations, we can live confidently within time. But what is good at the start can become dangerous when routine *replaces* life.

When *everything* becomes planned and regular, there is no room for surprises. Each day is identical to the previous one. We entrust our life to an autopilot system that only has to apply, as mechanically as possible, the preestablished instructions. The senses fall asleep. We no longer see each morning as a new day, each moment as a new beginning. Our sleepy eyes see only repetition. Without realizing it, we become what the psalm says of idols:

> They have mouths, but do not speak;
> eyes, but do not see.
> They have ears, but do not hear;
> noses, but do not smell.
> They have hands, but do not feel. (Ps 115: 5–7)

We may pretend it's possible to live like this. But there comes a time when, as the Book of Ecclesiastes says, "the eye is not satisfied with seeing, / or the ear filled with hearing" (Eccl 1:8). Routine does not fill the human heart. The great challenge is to look at everything, every day, with a fresh eye, to be dazzled by the surprises of our days, to recognize that this passing moment is the door through which joy enters.

For that to happen, we need to rediscover a sensitivity to life, to its disconcerting simplicity, to its fragile song, to its side roads— this life in which we become used to barely noticing a lightning bolt or the striking of a match. To be able to answer the question of the meaning of our lives, the question that each of us must at some point face, it is essential to reactivate our senses.

EXCESS COMMUNICATION

Besides each of us being a body, we are also members of a social body that supports, widens, or represses our sensitivity. Marshall McLuhan, the great communication theorist of the twentieth century, explained well how this reality is exploited by the global network of communications, which threatens the uniqueness of the person. What McLuhan said about television, for example, is very enlightening: "One of the effects of television is to destroy personal identity. By just watching TV, people become a collective group of identical individuals. They lose interest in the uniqueness of a person."

If we pay attention, we'll notice that contemporary means of communication (from television to telephone, from email to social networks) rely only on the two senses that perceive signals from a distance: sight and hearing. The result has been a disproportionate reliance on the eyes and ears. Gradually, these two senses come to bear all the responsibility for our connection with reality: "Did you see that?" "Have you heard the latest about...?" We are continually bombarded by the pressure of what we must see and hear. The same thing happens when it comes to transportation. Whether it's driving a car, walking the sidewalks of a big city, or piloting an airplane, the most essential senses are those that collect visual or auditory information. This is not the case in all cultures.

This overload of the senses that perceive what is furthest from us hides the underdevelopment and the need for the other senses. We have become less able to distinguish the scent of flowers. Although shopping the fruit and vegetable aisle of an odorless supermarket is surely a hundred times more convenient, it is not the same as walking through the cathedral of aromas that one experiences at an orchard or a garden.

It is the same with the other senses that call for proximity: taste and touch. Today, only professionals risk blind tastings. It is more and more the eyes that eat, through the elaborate presentation of plates, the refinement of the design, or the manipulation of the taste itself. Then there's touch. We are so separated from nature that we no longer know basic sensations like walking barefoot, relaxing in a field, gently spreading the leaves to clear a spring and drink slowly, or caressing the fragile life around us.

We thus become the "emotional illiterates" that the filmmaker Ingmar Bergman said we are. Isn't it time to come back to our senses? Isn't this a good time to revitalize them? Hasn't the time come to better understand the connection between the senses and meaning?

TOUCHING THE WORLD

Since classical antiquity, touch has often been considered the first of the senses (although Aristotle put it third on his list). Touch certainly has primacy in the order of creation. For the developing human, it is the sense that develops first in the womb. After birth, too, it is through physical contact that we understand reality: cold and hot, soft and hard, familiar and unfamiliar, discomfort and comfort. The infant recognizes all objects through touch; she inevitably takes them in her hands and brings them to her mouth. We can say that the sense of touch is our "first eye."

Our whole body is covered with skin, from head to toe. It separates us from the external world at the same time it connects us with it. The skin perceives texture, density, weight, and temperature. The sense of touch even puts us in relation to time and memory: through the impressions transmitted to us by touch, we make endless journeys without which we would not be who we are. Thanks to touch, we don't just stand in the presence of others; we *encounter* people.

In this sense, the question that Jesus asked in the midst of a dense crowd remains significant: "Who touched me?" (Mark 5:31). The disciples tried in vain to correct him, pointing out that he was being pressed on all sides by a crowd of people, but Jesus knew there is touch and then there is touch.

Rainer Maria Rilke wrote,

> Hands are a complicated organism, a delta into which many divergent streams of life rush together in order to pour themselves into the great storm of action. There is a history of hands; they have their own culture, their particular beauty; one concedes to them the right of their own development, their own needs, feelings, caprices and tendernesses.[11]

What Rilke says here about the hands can also be said about the skin. The story of our life is a story of skin and touch, of how we touch or don't touch, how we are touched or not touched. This story is told, for the most part, in our depths, without us thinking about it. Despite everything, it has so much to teach us. There is a mode of knowledge that is only accessible to us by touch, not only in infancy, but throughout our life.

The Catalan painter Miró always spoke of the tactile origin of his work. When he was young, in Barcelona, he studied under the architect Francisco Gali, who, though a classical academic, was willing to take unexpected paths in teaching his students. Miró admitted that he was not gifted at drawing and said his teacher had taught him to understand objects with his fingers and not just with his eyes by blindfolding him. Gali had Miró, while blindfolded or with closed eyes, pick up an object, feel it, turn it over in his hands, and then draw it. Miró said he became incapable of representing the world in any other way.

REDISCOVERING TASTE

Whether we like it or not, we have inherited theories that suggested a hierarchy of dignity among the various senses. St. Thomas Aquinas distinguished the superior from the inferior senses. The most spiritual and perfect sense was sight; hearing was also superior. These two, Aquinas said, are more closely associated with the mind, the intellect, the soul. Touch, smell, and taste were lower senses because they are more material, more corporeal. Of these, taste seems the lowest because it confines its activity to the mouth.

There are five basic categories of taste: bitter, sweet, salty, sour, and *umami*. The latter is the most recent category, the term officially recognized only in 1985 and still unfamiliar to most people. *Umami* (a Japanese loanword) means "savory." *Umami* has a sweet but lasting aftertaste, difficult to describe but completely identifiable. According to some, it makes flavors rounder. The next time you go to a Japanese restaurant, ask about it.

Jean-Jacques Rousseau reminds us of a great truth: "We are indifferent to a thousand things, as objects of touch, of hearing, or of sight; but there is almost nothing to which our sense of taste is indifferent."[12] In the virgin forest of Feuerbach's thought, we find an expression of rare transparency: "the gospel of the senses." Challenging the traditional separation between superior and inferior senses in terms of their cognitive qualities, Feuerbach argued that in the human person, taste rises to the dignity of a scientific and spiritual act.

Although its importance as one of the senses has long been disregarded, today we understand that taste has played a major role in the development of the human species. According to Richard Wrangham, a primatologist at Harvard University, cooking allowed our ancestors to triple their brain size. Cooking, he says—and, by that very fact, the sense of taste—made possible intellectual achievements such as cave paintings, the composition of great symphonies, and the invention of the internet.[13]

This new appreciation of the sense of taste marks an important shift. We have become aware of the need for a more global wisdom, based not solely on the mind, but on the total reality of the body that we are. We should not think of wisdom drawn from daily experiences such as taste as trivial, but as capable of giving us greater understanding of ourselves. One of our most basic abilities is the capacity to taste. There is an essential link between *knowledge* and *flavor*,[14] confirmed by their Latin etymology: *sapere*, *sapore*. The great teacher Ruben Alves used to say that "to enter a school (of thought), students and teachers should first go through the kitchen" and learn that flavor, like taste, is an art of desire.

THE POWER OF SMELL

The sense of smell is a great path to knowledge, but it is very subtle. It works through intimate contact with the world. Through it we receive information that emerges from living things, objects, or environments that cannot be conveyed by speech, noise, or action. An odor is very different from an image. With an image, the relationship between subject and object is of the order of representation, while with scent, what we perceive clings to us, enters us. An image we see tells us about an object outside of us; when our sense of smell perceives a scent, it's already upon and within us.

By the end of its first week of life, a newborn baby recognizes its mother by smell. It also happens that many years later, mothers still feel nostalgia for the unique smell of their baby. One of the most emblematic phrases of Pope Francis's first apostolic exhortation is his insistence that pastors must "take on the 'smell of the sheep.'"[15] We all understand what he meant by that.

Some architects argue that we underestimate the impact of odors on our perception of space. Places have an olfactory personality that is important to take into account because our sense of smell draws on our memories and affections for our habitat of origin. Even if it is negative, smell represents a heritage. How often does olfactory information unexpectedly bring back a memory from the depths of our unconscious—our childhood home, an old closet, a toy, a train station, a person we love?

Regarding this phenomenon, the philosopher Walter Benjamin said that the memory of a smell may be the most powerful kind of memory. It can be uniquely comforting, taking us into the past like few other memories are able. "A scent may drown years in the odor it recalls," he wrote.[16] When our olfactory capacities atrophy, the living cartography of our emotions also declines. Our brain can recognize almost a thousand different smells, a palette that is further enriched by the mixing of aromas and odors, each awakening in us sensations that language is not always able to describe. This makes our sense of smell crucial to our lives.

The German verb for "to seek or search," *suchen*, is related to the sense of smell. It comes from the vocabulary of hunters, and it suggests looking for something that one has initially perceived through smell. Perhaps God's own "smell" helps lead us to him. St. Bonaventure, in one of his works, speaks of the "odorous vestiges" of Christ. And in a beautiful poem called "O cheiro de Jesús" (The Smell of Jesus), the Portuguese poet Adília Lopes ends with these lines:

> Without limits
> or borders
> (without roof
> with a tile)
> is the smell of Jesus.

LISTEN!

The world around us is full of sounds, and the human ear perceives only a part of this immensity. Infrasound is low-frequency sound—below twenty hertz, the lowest we can hear. Although a human can't hear it, an elephant does easily—and without having to put its ear to the ground, because an elephant perceives sound waves through its legs, too! Meanwhile, ultrasonic sounds are those higher than twenty thousand hertz, the highest frequency we can perceive, but a dog or cat can hear frequencies twice as high. Also, if you think rock music is loud, what about the blue whale, which emits sounds that are audible hundreds of miles away? There is no doubt that the diversity of sounds is a world in itself, much of which remains mysterious to us.

With our ears, we listen to the outside world—noises, voices, the music that consoles us. When it comes to selfless listening to the other, however, there is another level of hearing that we need to learn. There is an important kind of listening that demands more than our ears; there is also listening with the heart, a deeper listening in which all the senses come into play. The Bulgarian-French philosopher Julia Kristeva speaks of an "infra-language," linked to the body, biology, and passions, and an "ultra-language," which encompasses history, present ideas, and the future—and all of these elements are aspects of listening.

Judaism and Christianity are listening religions. "Hear, O Israel..." (Deut 6:4) is how the fundamental prayer *Shema Yisrael* begins. "Let anyone with ears listen!" (Matt 11:15; 13:9, 43; Rev 2:7) is a New Testament refrain that punctuates the Christian canon.

One who says "listen" then offers something to listen to. What is that in this case? Perhaps, to borrow Clarice Lispector's words, it is this: "Hear me. Hear my silence. What I say is never what I say but instead something else....It captures that other thing that I'm really saying because I myself cannot."[17]

SEEING AND BEING SEEN

Light travels at the dizzying speed of 186,282 miles per second. It is to this hurried traveler that we owe the activation of the sophisticated mechanism that allows an eye to see. It is good to remember that sight is not only a sense, but the synthesis of many senses—it senses light intensity, colors, depth, distance, and more. It gathers an endless and dazzling collection of information. I recall the comment by the Italian poet Tonino Guerra, an agnostic who acknowledged that, like believers, agnostics have doubts, and that nothing caused him to doubt his own agnosticism more than consideration of the utter miracle that is *an eye*. The thought left him helpless at the gates of mystery.

Sight allows us to perceive the world around us, but the gaze has other equally fundamental dimensions, starting with that of reflectivity: our body, which sees all things, can also look at itself. It sees and is seen at the same time. Merleau-Ponty wrote,

> If our eyes were made so that not one part of our body could fall within our purview…or simply if we had lateral eyes that do not produce an overlapping of the visual fields as some animals do—such a body, unable to reflect upon itself, would then be incapable of feeling itself; such a body almost as rigid as stone, which would not quite be flesh, could not be the body of a man, and would be devoid of humanity.[18]

Seeing is fundamental to encountering ourselves and others. Looking at and recognizing the other who is before us helps us to love people for themselves. In the same way, seeing is essential for the adventure of the search for the meaning of life.

One of the most important theological treatises on sight is *On the Vision of God* (*De vision Dei*), by the fifteenth-century German theologian and bishop Nicholas of Cusa. This work grew from correspondence between its author and the monks of Tegernsee Abbey. Its purpose was to offer the monks a reflection on the ineffable gaze of God. This is how Nicholas describes God's gaze:

The angle of your vision, O God, is not quantum but infinite. It is also a circle, or rather, an infinite sphere because your sight is an eye of sphericity and of infinite perfection. Your sight sees all things simultaneously around and above and below....You are visible by all creatures and you see all. In that you see all you are seen by all. For otherwise creatures cannot exist since they exist by your vision. If they did not see who you see, they would not receive being from you. The being of a creature is equally your seeing and your being seen.[19]

Nicholas's words make clear the importance, not only of God's gaze, but of our own gaze—even if, as St. Paul says, "Now we see in a mirror, dimly" (1 Cor 13:12).

THE PROJECT OF SPIRITUALITY

In a magnificent essay called "The Aesthetics of Silence," Susan Sontag begins with an unexpected sentence that catches our attention: "Every era has to reinvent the project of 'spirituality' for itself."[20] Of course, "reinventing for itself" doesn't mean creating from scratch. It is a question of looking again from a new angle, of finding new ways of understanding, of risking a new synthesis. It is a matter of proposing—beginning from the act of believing but also from the act of living—a new grammar of wisdom. There is no lack of models—as we can verify in St. Paul's letter to Titus, one of the treasures of the Christian canon: "For the grace of God has appeared, bringing salvation to all, training us to renounce impiety and worldly passions, and in the present age to live lives that are self-controlled, upright, and godly" (Titus 2:11–12).

A mysticism of the present moment demands that we take more seriously the fact that in our humanity we can discover God living "in the present age."

We must look at spirituality as an integral part of being human. We often observe in ourselves a certain illiteracy before the fundamental expressions of life. We have certainties and experience and knowledge, but there are moments in life that leave us without words, before which we feel disoriented—an illness, a reversal of fortune, a crisis, or even a great joy, a great encounter. In certain circumstances, we embark on a new path, because our faith seems to be unable to account for all that we are or what we become. Dietrich Bonhoeffer, a great believer, wrote, "Being a Christian does not mean being religious in a certain way, making oneself into something or other (a sinner, penitent, or saint) according to some method or other. Instead, it means being human, but the human being Christ creates in us."[21]

What we are lacking today are not only teachers of "the interior life," but teachers of life as a whole, teachers who help us understand how to lead a life worth living. We need guides and witnesses of the human heart, its infinite and arduous paths, but also guides and witnesses of daily life, where everything is not extraordinarily simple and yet, at the same time, is. We need a new grammar that concretely reconciles things what our culture holds to be irreconcilable: reason and sensitivity, effectiveness and emotions, individuality and social engagement, sound leadership and compassion, spirituality and meaning, now and eternity. Out of the instantaneousness of our sense perceptions, can we develop an authentic mysticism? There is no doubt about it: what has already been said is not all there is to say.

A NEW RELATIONSHIP WITH TIME

One of the most important aspects of a true mysticism of the present moment must be renewing our relationship with time.

There is perhaps nothing that causes us more pain than time. Like a maker of traps who becomes ensnared in the product he built, we invented time, but we never have enough of it. Our clocks never sleep. How often do we complain that we have no time to relax or to develop ourselves? Convinced that we don't have enough time, we don't even try to live fully in the present moment. Like Cronus from Greek mythology, who devoured those he cared for, time consumes us without really leading us to the fulfillment of the promise. In this sense, the frantic race for material consumption is nothing more than an avid quest for compensation. The things we acquire are obviously much more than things—they are promises that capture our eye, an impotent protest against an existence that does not satisfy us, the fictions of our interior theater, a race against time.

The truth is that we must come to terms with time. A linear, uninterrupted, mechanized, purely historical conception of time is not enough. The homogeneous continuum of time conveyed by the theory of progress does not allow for the inbreaking of something new, something surprising. Salvation itself is just such a novelty. We need to discern in the present moment a double meaning: the present can be a horizontal, quantitative journey, lived as the progression between this moment and the one that will follow it; but the present also bears a vertical dimension that gives a new dimension to time by opening it up to eternity. It is this qualitative dimension of time that brings epiphany.

In the biblical tradition, we learn as much about God's creative activity as we do about God's rest. Something that causes us great problems is our inability to understand the meaning of this rest. God rested on the seventh day and in doing so brought the work of creation to completion. Without this rest, this *shabbat*, the action is not finished, not complete. This is what prompted Abraham Joshua Heschel to say about Saturday, the weekly day of rest for the Jews,

The meaning of the Sabbath is to celebrate time rather than space. Six days a week we live under the tyranny of

21

things of space; on the Sabbath we try to become attuned to *holiness in time*. It is a day on which we are called upon to share in what is eternal in time, to turn from the results of creation to the mystery of creation; from the world of creation to the creation of the world.[22]

We really need to rediscover the meaning of Saturday or Sunday. The body needs not only activity, but also rest. It must be freed from the pressure of the immediate, from the weight of tasks, by opening up to free moments, like the poet Angelus Silesius said of the rose: it is "without why"—it blooms because it blooms. Finally, we must find time to contemplate, to find delight in sounds and tastes, to breathe in the scent, and to touch what is around us.

DISCOVERING THAT WE ARE LOVED

There is more to breathing, to living, than mechanically bringing air in and out of our lungs; it means coexisting, living in a state of love. In the same way, embracing the mystery means entering into even our emotions. God—both all-powerful and fragile, impassible and capable of suffering, transcendent and loving, supernatural and within our grasp—can be found in our emotions. The madness of the Christian faith is not found in metaphysical affirmations; it is quite simply faith in the resurrection of the flesh.

Love is the true arouser of the senses. The various pathologies of the senses that we have mentioned above show us how much our vitality withers when love is absent. One of the most serious crises of our time is the disengagement of knowledge from love; a mysticism of the senses reveals knowledge that is accessible only by loving. To love means to open up, to break the circle of isolation, to live the miracle of being fully with ourselves and with the other. Love is the breaking of barriers. It is a form of hospitality, as the Brazilian poet Mario Quintana writes, "There is love when people live within one another."

But those who want to live in this way must let themselves be exposed, to be disarmed. Those who love are more vulnerable. They cannot pretend. If they want to sing in the street, they sing. If it occurs to them to run and laugh under a downpour, they do. If it occurs to them to dance in the middle of the street, they start to spin, without feeling in the least embarrassed, listening to music that others fail to hear. Love also exposes us to a greater intensity of suffering. Love renews our interest in life and makes us take it head-on. As a result, we more often come up against its mysterious dialectic: its extraordinary vitality and its terrible proximity to death. However, as the novelist Antonio Lobo Antunes wrote, "There is only one way never to suffer: it is never to love." What squelches life is not the inevitable suffering that accompanies love; rather, it is the opposite—apathy, distraction, selfishness, cynicism.

Love is the path that leads us to hope. Hope is not a self-comforting expectation of better days. It's even less about awaiting what's going to happen. Hope does not mean looking to a hypothetical future. It is knowing how to recognize the invisible at the heart of the visible, the indescribable at the heart of the audible, and so on. It is discovering another dimension within and beyond this concrete reality that is given to us in the present. All of our senses are called upon to welcome, with admiration and delight, the promise that comes and that is not only for an indefinite future, but already for today, at every moment. Hope keeps us alive. It protects us from being devoured by discouragement, absorbed by disillusionment, overthrown by the forces of death. To understand that hope flourishes in the present moment is to experience the scent of eternity.

A MYSTICISM WITH OPEN EYES

Early Christian art often depicts people at prayer. The way they are represented reminds us of the importance of the body in the act of faith. They are typically depicted standing, face up, arms outstretched, and eyes wide open. We pray with our bodies, not just our thoughts. Prayer inhabits each of our senses. This is why the desert fathers said that to open your hands, even before speaking a word, is already to pray. If gestures are a way of relating and communicating, it can only be so. It is the same with all the other senses. So we might also say that "opening your eyes is already to pray."

When, in his *Morals*, St. Basil of Caesarea asks what makes a Christian different, the first part of his answer is this: "To keep watch every day and at all hours." Vigilance means making the effort required to pay attention. It's not just an activity; it's a dynamic interaction of the heart and the senses. It is the opposite of distraction, which weakens our ability to live fully in the present moment. The mysticism of open eyes is not addressed to a distant God. Rather, it lives in the awareness of standing permanently before God. "Where can I go from your spirit? / Or where can I flee from your presence?" (Ps 139:7), the Psalmist asks God. In fact, if it happens that we do not see God, it is not because God is too distant, but rather that God is so close: "For 'In him we live and move and have our being'" (Acts 17:28).

We should also keep in mind that all the creatures around us are immersed at the same time as we are in the presence of God. This strongly commits us at the ethical level. If we love God, our love embraces the whole world. We love God through God's creatures, which are the expression of God's own love. For this reason, there is no spirituality with open eyes without an ecological and cosmic sense. This is reflected in Paul's letter to the Romans: "We know that the whole creation has been groaning in labor pains until now; and not only the creation, but we ourselves, who have the first fruits of the Spirit, groan inwardly while we wait for adoption, the redemption of our bodies" (Rom 8:22–23).

A mysticism of the present moment is a declaration of love for life and a commitment to building a common future.

WHAT *MYSTICISM* MEANS

Most works on mysticism published today are unfortunately limited to describing its historical character. They present it as a relic of the past, never describing what it is and means universally, but always in terms of a few historical figures: Hadewijch, Hildegard of Bingen, Teresa of Avila, and John of the Cross.

If I were given a moment, and only a moment, to explain the meaning of the word *mystic*, I would borrow the words of Michel de Certeau: A mystic is someone "who cannot stop walking."[23] I know that this expression, by its radical minimalism, may seem too simplistic in view of the complexity and the historical weight acquired by the concept of "mysticism." Nor does it do justice to Michel de Certeau himself, who, in the abundance and complexity of his writings, has clearly established that mysticism must be patiently developed over the course of a long process. Still, even long journeys must start with a small step, and that's what I'm pointing to here. Notice that this description of a mystic—one who cannot stop walking—includes one essential quality: it excludes no one. It testifies that mysticism is for everyone, that it is literally universal. This is important because this is not how mysticism is usually perceived, and that's a mistake.

Mysticism has long been considered to be the experience of a few, a marginal and elite path, disconnected from the concrete lives of most people and from the concerns and struggles of everyday life. But the writings of figures such as Merton, Certeau, or Raimon Pannikar have revolutionized our understanding. For the latter, mysticism is simply an "integral experience of life," and the mystic is one who lives by being open to all of reality, attentive and responsive to the pain of the world. A hunger and thirst for justice has a real place in the heart of a mystic, but the mystic does not allow herself to be caught up by one stage or aspect of the journey. Her spirituality is one of ambivalence: she is both embodied and committed, while being truly detached and free. Mysticism must always be synonymous with freedom. It is an immense freedom—free from everything, from everyone, from oneself—that requires an understanding of the interdependence between the infinitely small and the infinitely large, the near and the far, interior and exterior, ourselves and others, activity and rest, silence and speech, stillness and movement, stability and exploration, spring and winter, hunger and bread, now and later.

The mystic is one who cannot stop moving forward. Aware of what she lacks, she perceives that each step of the way is only temporary, and she continues to aspire to something more. As Michel de Certeau reminds us, the mystic "lives nowhere"; she is "inhabited."[24] Like the Greek king Ulysses, the mystic is tied to the mast of hope—not a hope in the future, but in the invisible, that is, the not yet visible.

ONE OR THE OTHER?

An unusual correspondence between two friends, the writer Romain Rolland and the founder of psychoanalysis Sigmund Freud, on the subject of mysticism sheds light on many of the preconceived ideas and misunderstandings that flourish today. Rolland was reacting to something Freud had written in his book *The Future of an Illusion* (1926). According to Freud, it is an illusion to think that we can find elsewhere (and by "elsewhere," he primarily means religion) the answers that science cannot give us. According to him, religious images are only fictions that express the infantile need for the all-powerful protection of a father. Rolland rejects this radical psychological reduction by noting "the simple and direct fact" that "religious sentiment" is a real and inalienable experience; it is the "feeling of the 'eternal'" that nothing can destroy, the (admittedly subjective) "sensation" experienced by millions of people, the rich and vital "oceanic" feeling that is the very expression of life or, better still, of its essence.[25] To these ideas, Freud responded, "How remote from me are the worlds in which you move! To me mysticism is just as closed a book as music."[26]

Here we see two seemingly irreconcilable points of view. For Rolland, the fundamental point of constructing the personality is the discovery of the unity with the world that lies within each person's consciousness, while Freud considers this fundamental point to be the recognition of a generative division of the self. The key question is this: How long will we consider "unity" or "division" to be an impossible choice?

Certainly, the analytical cartography of the human person drawn by Freud and the human sciences cannot be purely and simply tossed into the trash, in favor of some idealized unity, in which we are diluted like drops in the ocean of God. We would be deluding ourselves. It would be a reductionist isolationism and a positivist pretension to consider that reality in all its complexity (the world and ourselves) can only be deciphered by reason. We must open our eyes to the wisdom that is offered to us in the present moment. The next moment is unknown to us. Unless the only remaining alternative is the conclusion reached by Macbeth—that life is just "a tale told by an idiot, full of sound and fury, signifying nothing"?

Mysticism, understood as an integral experience of life, challenges us to recognize and maintain the tensions—matter and spirit, body and soul, reason and feeling—in harmony. It is not a question of denying them, nor of fusing them together.

A NAKED EXPERIENCE

I like twentieth-century philosopher Georges Bataille's description of what he called "atheist mysticism," because it also works well as a description of Christian mysticism. Mysticism, he says, is "a naked experience." First, his definition is right because it roots mysticism in the realm of *experience*. The great resistance of many people to mysticism arises from the fact that so many others have used it to justify a flight from reality. This is precisely the opposite of the words that the author of the New Testament's letter to the Hebrews puts in the mouth of Christ: "Sacrifices and offerings you have not desired, / but a body you have prepared for me" (Heb 10:5).

Mysticism has concreteness. It is body, experience, place, living tissue. Most of the time, what is missing from the believer's faith is not ideas, not truths, but corporeality, resonance, weight. This path is not described only by concepts or structures. The precariousness and fragility of the body, the cry, universal and concrete, that springs from it, its common and daily breathing brings us closer to God more than any conceptual elaboration can.

Nevertheless, we must not lose sight of the fact that mystical experience is a "naked experience"; it is marked by vulnerability. An experience of faith requires *trust*, not a guarantee. Faith does not possess what it believes in, because the object of faith is always *alter*, "other." As Michel de Certeau writes,

> When approaching the One they love, believers always experience, in one way or another, a feeling of emptiness: they embrace a shadow! They expect to meet him by approaching him, but he is not there. They look for him everywhere, they scan every corner where he could be. But he's nowhere.[27]

Mystics know very well that God is revealed in hiddenness. Between God and us, there is an empty space. We explore this space. The essential is beyond, but it is only in the poverty of our flesh and our time, which are also the flesh and time of God, that we can recognize God, see God, encounter God, and experience God in the transparency of the moment. God does not run away from the mundane and the ordinary but embraces all that is delicious and difficult on our journey. We can thus read as a prayer the verse of the poet Sophia de Mello Breyner Andresen: "I believe in the nudity of life." As difficult and tortuous as it can turn out to be, there is no more lucid and transparent way to begin our spiritual life.

THE SACRAMENT OF THE PRESENT MOMENT

Fernando Pessoa wrote, "Blessed are the moments and the millimeters and the shadows of little things."[28]

In a sort of spiritual testament, the theologian Karl Rahner offered the famous observation that "the Christian of the future will be a mystic, or he will not exist at all."[29] According to Rahner, the contemporary believer's faith will have two main features. On one hand, the believer's spirituality needs to be lived continuously in the first person, which inevitably requires an awakening of consciousness. On the other hand, the believer is called to the courage of a decision of faith in the Holy Spirit, a decision that finds its strength in itself and that is the effective proof of a personal experience of God.

Now, *the mystical intersection of divine history and human history is the present moment*—not an idealized or abstract moment, but this concrete moment. It is this precious minute in which we are, this concrete hour of our life, this day that our heart faces with more or less hope. It is this moment that can inform us of what is imminent; what is approaching, whether predictable or unpredictable; what is coming, in obvious or very discreet form.

Fr. Joseph Marie Perrin, a Dominican and a great confidant of Simone Weil, said that nothing we know is more like eternity than the present moment and that we should symbolically understand it as a sacrament, the eighth sacrament. We who enter and leave the temples must also venerate the admirable holiness of the present moment! Perrin wrote,

> One who doesn't know how to rest
> inside a moment
> will never know that serene
> and enlightened peace
> of "being-with."

If we take a good look, we see that we are continuously stripped of the past and, whatever we do, we cannot anticipate the smallest bit of the future, however small. We only have the present moment. Only the present moment belongs to us. Between the infinite possibilities of divine love and the changing and progressive experience of the human in us, the only point of contact is the present moment. It is the clay from which life takes shape and is discovered. It is the fragile rope bridge that unites time and promise.

We receive confirmation of this in this wonderful and challenging poem by Thérèse de Lisieux:

> My life is but an instant, a passing hour,
> My life is but a day that escapes and flies away.
> O my God! You know that to love you on earth
> I have only today![30]

The mysticism of the present moment thus returns us to an authentic existence by teaching us to become really present—to see in each tiny thing a parcel of infinity, to hear in each sound the echo of eternity, to touch the intangible in the simplest gestures, to savor the splendid banquet in what is frugal and scarce, and to get drunk on the scent of the ever new flower of the present moment.

PART TWO

A THEOLOGY OF THE SENSES

INTRODUCTION

The Christian tradition includes a rich theology of the senses, but the word *senses* has too often been given a primarily *spiritual* meaning—concepts that normally relate to the body are applied instead to the soul. The so-called natural senses were the faculties of the body to perceive terrestrial things, while spiritual senses were described as the soul's abilities to grasp divine realities.

The first theoretician of this current of thought was Origen of Alexandria in the first half of the third century; he emphatically defended the idea that the spiritual senses became more sensitive when a person *separated* and purified himself from his *bodily* experience.[1] This was the main idea, which is not to say that this theology of the spiritual senses didn't include, in Origen himself and those who developed his thought, more nuance and complexity that was genuinely insightful.

But the basic paradigm of this theology was to cast the relationship between natural and spiritual senses mainly in terms of opposition, and this is still partly the case today. Developing one's spiritual life was more a matter of *separating* oneself from the bodily senses than of *unifying* the bodily with the spiritual. It is true, nevertheless, that from antiquity to the present day, some theologians have qualified this point of view, making some effort to move in another direction. In medieval scholasticism, for example, St. Bonaventure stands out with an original, unified anthropology, developing a resolutely positive vision of the bodily senses. Some say that the history of the West would not have been the same if Bonaventure's philosophy had prevailed. It may be true.

The truth is that today more than ever we are faced with a need to make connections, a dialogue between the wisdom of faith and the wisdom of life. We need to rediscover, from faith, an understanding of the human person; we also need, starting from the person, a new understanding of faith. Indeed, there are not the spiritual senses on one hand and the natural senses on the other. Nor can one truly speak of the spiritual life or spiritual journey without proceeding by analogy. There is *life*; it is unique and whole.

Carl Jung wrote, "It seems to me that the one who does the will of God is the person who seeks to realize his human nature and not the one who flees from it." Our humanity is always spiritual or, at the very least, it always holds this possibility within itself, because God does not knock on a door that is not present in us. The door God knocks on is one we can open because it is part of who we are. "Listen! I am standing at the door, knocking; if you hear my voice and open the door, I will come in to you and eat with you, and you with me," says the Book of Revelation (3:20). God comes to meet us through the most daily, the most commonplace, the closest door: our five senses. They are the great entrances and exits of our living humanity. Let us learn to recognize them as theological sources, that is, as privileged places of the manifestation of God and of our relationship with God.

In the following pages, we will suggest a way of *embracing one's bodily senses* as part of developing in oneself an authentic *mysticism of the present moment*. The approach will be fragmentary, incomplete, and provisional. These are merely reflections, not an exhaustive and deep study. They are snapshots, not a panoramic topographical map. "In my Father's house there are many dwelling places" (John 14:2).

With this in mind, the reflections that make up each of the five sections of this part of the book include texts of various kinds: biblical commentary and brief scientific remarks, philosophical texts and poetry that made an impression on me. There is anthropology, literature, cinema, and some biographical notes in a style that invites reflection, but one that also wants to challenge and prompt a response. Most of what follows is published here for the first time, but some parts have been published previously and I integrated them because of their obvious connection with the topic at hand. It is a topic I have been interested in for a long time, and in that sense, I suppose I began writing this book long ago.

1

TOUCHING WHAT ESCAPES US

TOUCH, ONLY TOUCH

At a certain stage of our existence, we realize that the essential questions of life can only be confronted from within our human condition, played out in this precarious, unsettled place that always seems so incomplete, always more unexplainable than we would like, in this mixture of clay and breath that we are. There comes a time in life when a small voice without words reaches us at the most living and most singular point of our existence. This voice tells us nothing, does not transmit any message to us. If we question it, it offers no statement.

Our first stage of learning necessarily involves speaking, but that's not the case here. We feel touched—only touched. This comes to us through an experience of great joy or great pain, through extreme fatigue or a question that demands to be answered, through a desire to give up or one to be reborn—in short, by a destabilizing shock.

GROPINGLY, AS THOUGH WE SEE THE INVISIBLE

To reflect on the nature of *faith*, I often turn to a painting by the artist Eugene Delacroix that depicts the patriarch Jacob's nocturnal encounter with an angel (see Gen 32:22–32). I come back to this painting regularly because I find in its visual theology a realism, lucidity, and consolation that is absent from most written theology. What Delacroix shows us is that, in the experience of faith, we make our own body vulnerable as God makes himself vulnerable, too; we touch and we are touched, in an encounter without protective armor or artifices. It demands our whole presence. This giving of presences, one to the other, God's and ours, establishes a common history in the present moment.

The painting also tells us that faith, even if portrayed as a journey toward enlightenment, is a nocturnal experience. Faith is necessarily a state of questioning, uncertainty, maturation, and journeying. It is not a matter of moving forward from evidence to evidence; it is a journey made gropingly, as though we see the invisible One, to paraphrase the beautiful and challenging passage from the Letter to the Hebrews (11:27). Finally, it shows us that the tension of faith is resolved in a promise, an embrace, a dance. It is not just a reality to someday be reached and attained in some great beyond; it's a reality that can be savored already, in the here and now.

MODES OF TOUCHING

It turns out that touch is the most visceral, the most fundamental, and the most delicate sense. It tells us what is on our skin and how much a single touch can contain—that it can hold the entire universe. Touch is indelible, and it is concrete. It is our body's border and its beginning; it is anonymous and ardently singular; it is specific and concise, but usually the duration of its resonance in us is incalculable. We can describe touch as a producer and decoder of messages that seduce or repel, interrupt or prolong, caress or keep at a distance. As the Finnish architect Juhani Pallasmaa reminds us, "All the senses, including vision, can be regarded as extensions of the tactile sense; the senses are specializations of skin tissue, and all sensory experiences are modes of touching and thus related to tactility."[1]

MY LIFE ONLY TOUCHES THE FRINGE

"No one has ever seen God" (1 John 4:12). We bear this comment of St. John like a wound. None of us has seen God. Despite everything, God's presence, the way God's love touches us, gives meaning to our life. This paradox, which is a source of hope, is not, however, a thorn. Most of the time, we only experience an encounter that seems not to have happened, the great silence of God. We seek God without seeing God, we believe in God without experiencing God, we listen for God's voice without really hearing it.

We grope for God's face in absence and silence, but despite everything, absence and silence, mysteriously, suggest a presence. In the Russian filmmaker André Tarkovsky's *Nostalghia*, there is a haunting scene in which we see a group of people walking without interacting, a multitude walking in all directions, as though in a labyrinth. We then hear a voice, the voice of the narrator breaking the silence with the cry, "But say something, Lord. Give them a word. They are seeking. Don't you see that it is you that they want?" The voice of God is then heard and replies, "If I say something, do you think they will be able to hear it?" That is the drama of the silence of God: the difficulty of bringing together the finite and the infinite, grace and freedom, the provisional and the definitive, now and tomorrow.

But we know that silence is not God. Silence is a place of struggle, seeking, and waiting. Little by little, we embrace the possibility of making space, of opening up our life to others, and of letting ourselves be inhabited by its revelation. To a large extent, the possibility of God inhabits us. In this sense, faith takes the form of a hypothesis. Faith is an expectation. It feeds on struggle because nothing is ever complete, ever finished, ever completely known. We move gropingly. The fact that God is so close to our history does not cancel out the dimension of agony and questioning that our existence carries. The life of the believer remains to be invented, to be built; it is still incomplete, always a place of turbulence, agitation, and reconfiguration.

The Portuguese writer Sophia de Mello Breyner Andresen put in the mouth of one of her characters, an astrologer-king, a prayer that he recited before questioning the stars:

> Lord, how far you are, hidden and present! I can't hear your silence coming towards me and my life only touches the limpid fringe of your absence. I scrutinize around me the solemnity of things like one tries to decipher some difficult writing. But it's you who read me and know me. Make sure that no part of my being is hidden. Call to your clarity the whole of my being so that my thought becomes transparent and can hear the word you have always spoken to me.[2]

GO DOWN TO THE POTTER'S HOUSE

Life is entirely tactile. You can't automate it, mass-producing experiences. Life requires the patience of the potter who, in order to make a vase that satisfies her, makes two hundred just to learn the process, acquire the skill, and develop her idea. Life requires the hope of one who makes and remakes, with confidence, in a succession of beginnings.

For this reason, let us not be surprised at what we are told in the Book of the prophet Jeremiah: "Come, go down to the potter's house, and there I will let you hear my words" (Jer 18:2). There is an aspect of God's word that can only be understood in a potter's house, that is, in the contemplation of the incessant work of an artist's hands, in their humble and timeless dance, working the earth like a prayer.

Writing about the sculptor Auguste Rodin—and a sculptor and a potter share similar skills—Rainer Maria Rilke commented that those who work with their hands better understand the need for silence. Is this why God sends us to the potter's house?

THE TOUCH OF JESUS

Peter's first great encounter with Jesus ends with a strange but insightful request. When Peter senses who Jesus is, he says to him, "Go away from me, Lord, for I am a sinful man!" (Luke 5:8). Instead of saying "Lord, save me!" (Matt 14:30), as he will do later during the episode of the storm on the lake, Peter expresses an awareness of his own unworthiness. Nevertheless, Jesus rejects the establishment of some kind of a sealed border, which would prevent any transformative experience from occurring, between the pure and the unclean, sin and grace. Unlike the Pharisaic tradition, which advocated the need for a zone of purity, Jesus touches the untouchable. He reaches out to those who are not supposed to touch or be touched.

In the next scene, the Gospel tells us about Jesus's healing of a leper. In a movement that is as existential as it is spatial, a man suffering from leprosy ignores the social boundaries his society imposed because of his disease and approaches Jesus saying, "Lord, if you choose, you can make me clean" (Luke 5:12). In the context of the time, a leper was expected to keep a distance from all people, including his or her family, to avoid the risk of contamination. He or she was obliged to cry out to anyone nearby to warn them, but this one comes forward to meet Jesus. He does it because he senses the openness of this prophet of Nazareth. Notice that in response to his request for healing, Jesus does not stop at answering, "I do choose"; he also extends his hand and *touches* the man (Luke 5:13).

Jesus could have simply sent the man to wash himself seven times in the waters of the Jordan River, like the Old Testament prophet Elisha had done (2 Kgs 5:10). He prefers instead to run the risk of contamination by touching the man's wound. He wanted to sympathize with the man's suffering in a way that only touch can do. Jesus's touch helped to overcome the ostracism internalized by the man's forced separation. What heals the leper? What heals the hemorrhaging woman, also considered unclean, who, in another episode of the Gospel, approaches Jesus from behind and touches him (see Luke 8:43–48)? They are healed by the power of God manifested in Jesus, certainly—but in a particular way. They heal because they are touched, for Jesus's touch signifies that they are encountered, accepted, recognized, redeemed, embraced. All distance is abolished. The touch of Jesus rebuilds our humanity.

FAITH IS A TACTILE RELATIONSHIP

In Jesus's day, when a person gave a banquet, very often he left the doors of his home wide open to satisfy social curiosity; even so, of course, a border remained. Guests who have the right to be inside the house is one matter; uninvited intruders are another.

In Luke, we read of an occasion when Jesus is invited to one of these meals at the home of a Pharisee, and a woman, whose name is not even given but who is known as a sinner, enters the house and comes to stand "behind him at his feet" (Luke 7:38)—the position of a disciple. This woman places herself in the entourage of Jesus, to depend on him. As she enters, the narration slows down. Her gestures are described in detail: she cries at his feet and sheds enough tears to make them wet; she wipes them with her hair, kisses them several times, anoints them with perfume—all without saying a word. But through this shocking way of touching Jesus, she already says so much! Jesus accepts what she has to say, even knowing that whoever accepts being touched by a sinner also becomes unclean and that in the eyes of the person who was hosting him at that moment, this would be very demeaning. In fact, seeing this, the Pharisee says to himself, "If this man were a prophet, he would have known who and what kind of woman this is who is touching him—that she is a sinner" (Luke 7:39).

Jesus takes advantage of this woman's singular touch to remind his host what true hospitality is:

> Do you see this woman? I entered your house; you gave me no water for my feet, but she has bathed my feet with her tears and dried them with her hair. You gave me no kiss, but from the time I came in she has not stopped kissing my feet. You did not anoint my head with oil, but she has anointed my feet with ointment. (Luke 7:44–46)

What *is* touching? Sometimes our life, even in its spiritual dimension, is like a dance in which we never touch nor allow anyone to touch us. We trust too much in *words*, thinking they are enough, that they are the only way one can "say" something. Yet this unnamed woman tells her story to Jesus without using a single word, thus testifying that faith is a tactile relationship.

Jacques Maritain left us this striking portrait, as disconcerting as it is evangelical, of the faith of the poet Charles Péguy: "He believes that the faith of the coalman is greater than the faith of Saint Thomas....Only things perceptible to the senses touch him."

THE SPIRIT OF JESUS

The Holy Spirit comes to shake the structures, to touch us in the deepest and the most intimate ways. The Spirit comes as a gesture from Jesus who rebuilds the house (see Acts 1:1–12). The Spirit is not content to remain external but is like the water that penetrates the earth to help it bloom. We need this breath that truly moves us, pushes us, touches us. The Holy Spirit is given for the foundations, as an outer covering. The Holy Spirit is not a communication operation, God's marketing tool. The Spirit marks our depths, stirs us where we did not think it was possible to reach, in the vital and secret core where everything in us is decided. Whoever receives the Spirit is caught up in the adventure of God. The Holy Spirit generates a new equilibrium and, for this reason, is disconcerting, surprising. However, this is how the Spirit opens us to new wisdom, new understanding, new gestures, new poetry.

It is not we who determine the movement of the Holy Spirit: it is the Spirit who touches us, the Spirit who instructs us. Sometimes it seems that if we could, we would develop a manual for the Spirit to follow. The temptation to instrumentalize God grips us and does not let us go. Yet the opposite is true: it is the Spirit who leads us, the Spirit who comes to rest like fire on each of us, and the Spirit who enkindles the fire capable of lighting up history.

We get used to laws engraved in stone, exterior and particularistic, so we are surprised when everyone hears the Spirit speaking in his or her own language. God speaks the language of each person in order to establish a new covenant in each heart. The Spirit comes, not to enact a catalogue of norms for us, but to reveal the deeper meaning of our life. Abundant and generous, without restrictions or boundaries, this is the gift of the Spirit.

TOUCHED BY HOPE

Michelangelo said the work he did in creating his sculptures was not an act of invention, but of liberation. He looked at a rough stone and recognized the exceptional statue it could become. That's why when talking about his work, Michelangelo said, "All I do is free it from the stone."

I am convinced that great creative works, whether they are artistic or simply human, arise from a similar process. It is an exercise in hope. Life, with a capital L, a life worthy of the name, is nothing more than an act of hope that, most of the time, is very risky. Without hope, we only see the stone, the raw appearance, an impenetrable obstacle. It is hope that lets us see what could be, that shows beyond the harsh present conditions the wealth of possibilities still hidden. Hope dialogues with the future and brings it closer. Our existence, from start to finish, is a profession of faith in hope.

Everything and everyone are a journey, an unfinished experience, a quest in incompleteness. Masterpieces do not arise from nothing. They are the fruit of patience and slow development, punctuated by unforeseen events and efforts, more filled with dark nights than clear mornings. But without hope, no masterpiece can exist. Michelangelo's sculptures, for example, were made of marble, of course, but also of great hope. The marble could be of greater or lesser quality, as evidenced by the famous slave sculptures that we can see at the Louvre; hope tells us that nothing is wasted. To bear fruit, the seed needs the farmer's hand to till the soil. The boat needs someone who, in love with the voyage, is willing to leave the tempting tranquility of the port. The blank page needs someone to risk telling a story. In the smallest things as in the big ones, we find the same call to hope.

45

THE LONELINESS THAT TOUCHES US

Contemporary culture no longer prepares us for loneliness. Most of the time, difficult circumstances force us to learn on our own, without any support, how to experience loneliness. It's as if loneliness were an absolute surprise in our human experience rather than what it actually is: an experience common to everyone. There is a comment by Truman Capote that I wrote down in my notebook many years ago: "We are all alone, under the sky, with those we love."

We forget that for everyone, even those who are emotionally balanced and those who live feverishly active lives, loneliness comes to visit. We are alone with ourselves and even when we're among others. We were alone during our childhood, during the flowing of youth, and during our adult life; we will be alone in our old age. Friendship and love are means of sharing and reducing loneliness, living it serenely, or infusing it with creativity; but even in the round embrace of lovers or the magnificent dance of friends, the unsettling hum of loneliness will continue to be heard, at least at times, in the background. With this in mind, we must humanize our expectations of life.

It is also for this reason that I prize the lucid words of the Brazilian writer Nélilda Pinon, who turned to meditation as a fundamental antidote to the contemporary appeal of anything that distracts us from ourselves: "Solitude sought is the place where I learned best to find myself."

LET YOURSELF BE TOUCHED

An Ingmar Bergman film portrays an anorexic girl. Her anorexia is depicted as a form of divestment from life that can serve as a symbol of so many other resignations. The girl goes to a doctor who says something like this, which is valid for us too: "Look, there is only one remedy for you. I see only one way out: let yourself be touched by someone or something every day."

THE SENSIBLE DISCOVERY OF GOD

It is quite possible that our problem is not an inadequate understanding of the dogmatic truth about the Holy Trinity, but an inadequate awareness of the Trinity in our deep motivations and in our way of life. The Trinity is not only a mystery of faith; it is also a truth to be put into practice, a path to follow, a gesture to make, a way of life to learn, a way of being to be revealed. In other words, faith in the Trinity must have visible consequences in us, touching us in a way that can be seen outwardly. This is the fruit of a long maturation: to understand that the Holy Trinity is the holy door through which we enter with our whole life, learning to move from duality to the trinitarian way.

Let us consider two episodes of the Gospel that, while they don't directly express faith in the Trinity (which is not, moreover, their subject), help us to draw nearer to its mystery and to translate it into living.

We start with the experience of the disciples of Emmaus (Luke 24:13–35). They simply welcome a companion who joins them half-way along their journey. They accept that he speaks to them and they listen to him. They allow him to open for them the meaning of the Scriptures and to communicate to their hearts a new ardor, and when they reach their destination, they invite him to share a meal. The paschal revelation that takes place during this Emmaus meal is the experience of *two becoming three*. As long as there were two of them, they could not understand the meaning of Jesus's death or see, in the empty tomb, anything other than an enigma offered by some women. It is when they welcome this third, when they go from two to three, that they discover the truth that Jesus is alive.

We tend to live dualities or dialectics: it's either me *with* the other or me *against* the other. But the living God is a community. The living God is not an isolated person, with whom I have a one-way relationship and who neither looks at anyone else nor crosses the boundaries of you and me. Trinitarian dynamism, on the contrary, is the expansive and inclusive movement of God. Being three guarantees universality. If we believe in the Trinity, it becomes the model for an open, inclusive, and shared life.

Gratuitous love, selfless love, love that seeks nothing in return is always a trinitarian love. When we say "God is love," we mean that God is the perfection of love. The Holy Trinity is not the face of an eccentric God who, instead of being one, is three. The Trinity is clear evidence, the simplest truth of all. There is a stage where love, to be true (or to continue to be true), must become trinitarian. It is trinitarian love that elevates love to the highest dimension of itself.

By way of example, let us consider a second Gospel passage, the parable of the prodigal son (Luke 15:11–32). We have read it many times, but have we ever considered that this story tells us the need to live a trinitarian dynamism? The youngest son leaves. The reasons for his decision are not given. Perhaps we can seek his motivations in the desire for autonomy that is the basis of personal identity. He needs space. He needs to take some risks. It is also true that his conduct shows us that his mistake was his individualistic vision of life, which left no room for the other in his field of vision and no consideration of the future: "The younger son gathered all he had and traveled to a distant country, and there he squandered his property in dissolute living" (Luke 15:13).

Upon his return, when his father receives him joyfully, the older brother refuses to enter the house. The father then goes to this older son and begs him: "Son, you are always with me, and all that is mine is yours. But we had to celebrate and rejoice, because this brother of yours was dead and has come to life; he was lost and has been found" (Luke 15:31–32).

What did the father tell him through these words? I suggest that his message is something like this: "My son, everything you do is good. You have always accomplished your task, you have been faithful to me, but, in truth, it is still little. Until now, you have lived a relationship in two, only between you and me, as if you were an only son. If you can't accept your brother who has returned, you don't understand what God's love is."

Faith is the sensible and practical discovery of a community of love.

GRATITUDE FOR WHAT WE ARE NOT GIVEN

We know we should be thankful for what we have been given. And there is no lack of reasons for gratitude. Obviously, what we have also depends in many ways on our own efforts and inventiveness, things that we have built and achieved over time, often through laborious and lonely work, including avoiding problems that might have threatened what we've done. Yet that doesn't change this basic fact: our lives are a gift. By pure gift, we have received the most precious good: existence. Likewise, without ever doing anything to "earn" it, we have experienced—and continue to experience—being protected, cared for, welcomed, and loved. If we were to list all that we receive from others (and it's a pity that we don't carry out an exercise like this more often), we would realize what the poet Adilia Lopes offers as a truth that she realized: "I am a work of others."

We all are. Our story began before we existed, and it will continue after we are gone. We are the result of a series of countless encounters, gestures, kindnesses, efforts, caresses, affections. Our lives have meaning and value that we don't create but only receive.

This is priceless and cannot be bought or earned: it is only achieved through gift. When we fail to recognize that meaning and value, or others fail to recognize or respect it in us, it marks our entire lives. The void it leaves can't be filled, even with the abundant and powerful industry of fantasies of all kinds.

One thing I've been realizing more recently, though, is the importance of what has *not* been given to us. It was an insight offered by a friend that helped me on this. My friend told me,

> I like to give thanks to God for all that he gives me; it's always so much goodness that I can't even find the words to describe it. But I feel like I also have to thank God for what he doesn't give me, good things that I don't have, even those that I've asked for repeatedly but never received. Not getting these things has forced me to discover strength in myself that I didn't know I had and, in a way, helped me to become myself.

This is so true! However, understanding this requires a radical transformation of our inner attitude. Becoming an adult interiorly is not exactly a quick or painless process. In the meantime, when we do not give thanks to God, to life, or to others for what they have *not* given us, it seems that our prayer remains incomplete. We can easily nurture a sense of resentment for what has not been given to us, compare ourselves with others, see ourselves as victims, and weep over our disappointment about all the ways our lives do not match the ideal that we've constructed for ourselves. Or we can look at what has not been given to us as an opportunity, albeit mysterious and "in reverse," to begin a path of deepening...and of resurrection.

At one of the darkest hours of the twentieth century, inside a concentration camp, Etty Hillesum managed to engage in one of the most admirable spiritual adventures of our time. She wrote in her journal,

The greatness of the human being, his true wealth, is not in what is seen, but in what he carries in his heart. The greatness of a man does not come from the place he occupies in society, nor from the role he plays in it, nor from his social success. All of this can be taken away from a person overnight. All of this can go away in no time. The greatness of a person is precisely what remains in him when all that gave him an outward glow has died out. And what is left? His interior resources and nothing else.

DID THOMAS TOUCH JESUS?

The conversation between the risen Jesus and the apostle Thomas that happened the week after Easter (John 20:24–29) has been the subject of reams of commentary, and yet it remains an enigma. The fact that we don't fully understand this text means we haven't tamed it; this text continues and will continue to elude us, intrigue us, and keep us turning back to it, with the newness of a first meeting or the density of feelings that persist between two old rivals.

What is the reason for the difficulty? When the other disciples tell Thomas that in his absence, they have seen the risen Lord, he answers, "Unless I see the mark of the nails in his hands, and put my finger in the mark of the nails and my hand in his side, I will not believe" (John 20:25). As a condition for believing, he insists on confirmation of the facts through two senses: he needs to *see* and *touch* the wounds. A week later, Jesus appears to them again and this time addresses Thomas, offering him the proof he demanded: "Put your finger here and see my hands. Reach out your hand and put it in my side. Do not doubt but believe" (v. 27). When Thomas replies, "My Lord and my God!" Jesus adds, "Have you believed because you have seen me? Blessed are those who have not seen and yet have come to believe" (vv. 28–29).

51

Part of the puzzle lies in this last sentence. Until that point in the story, two senses have been called upon: sight and touch. But now, in this final sentence of Jesus, it's all about sight. Moreover, Jesus praises believing without seeing. Where did touch go? Why has it disappeared from the conversation? One possible answer is that once Thomas saw Jesus standing before him and heard Jesus speak to him, he didn't need to go so far as to touch him, despite Jesus's invitation, in order to realize that it really was Jesus standing there—and so since Thomas did not touch Jesus, Jesus did not address the sense of touch. Is that what's going on here?

The question of touch arises again in another meeting of someone with the risen Christ. When Mary Magdalene encounters him in the garden near the tomb (John 20:11–18), Jesus says, "Do not hold on to me" (or "Do not touch me") (v. 17). The philosopher Jean-Luc Nancy wrote a curious essay on this passage, in which he argues that the expression "Do not touch me" places us—paradoxically—in the register of touch. In fact, saying "Do not touch me" doesn't just mean that, but more literally, "Do not wish to touch me" or "Do not even think of touching me."[3] More existentially, it means this: "Learn that touching love is nothing other than accepting the other who escapes us." It is to live without the consolation of the hyphen, to live in the space that separates the "I" and the "you," not as the separation of mourning, but as a paschal opening. We return to the question about Thomas: did he touch Jesus or not?

WHAT DO I LOVE WHEN I LOVE YOU?

What do we love when we love God? St. Augustine helps us to understand that the love of God passes through sensible things and is expressed in a sensory way—through the clarity of light, the enigmatic scent of flowers, the odors of the world, the sounds that surround us, manna and honey, the embraces of the flesh. The mystical life is not a state of impermeability; in fact, it's the opposite of that. It is a recognition of the radical *porosity* of life. It is a rhythm, a fatigue, a breath, a voice, a skin, a light and a shadow, a presence, a heartbeat, a crown of thorns, a wandering joy. It is a call to a living encounter of love. Let us listen, then, to Augustine of Hippo:

> What is it that I love when I love you? Not the beauty of outward appearance, nor the splendor of time, not the fairness of light (and look how pleasing that is to our eyes), not the dulcet melodies of all kinds of song, not the sweet scent of flowers and salves and perfumes, not manna and honey, not limbs which are fit for bodily embraces. It is not these things that I love when I love my God, and yet I love one particular light and one particular voice, and one particular scent, and one particular food, and one particular embrace when I love my God—the light, voice, scent, food, embrace of my inner being. There, something that no place can contain shines brightly before my soul, and there sound is heard that time does not carry away, and there scent is inhaled that no wind can disperse, and there taste is savored that greed cannot diminish, and there is an attachment that no surfeit can sunder. This is what I love, when I love my God.[4]

CHANGING HANDS

In a scene from a film by the Polish director Krzysztof Kieślowski, a character approaches a window at a particularly difficult time in his life, and he sees an old lady who is struggling up the street, carrying a shopping bag in each hand. As he watches her, he sees her stop for a moment, just a moment, to switch hands with her bags (the bag that was in her right hand goes to her left hand

and vice versa), as we often do ourselves when we carry heavy loads. Then the old lady resumes her walk. I wonder what Kieślowski's character is thinking about at this point; it also makes me wonder about what we see, what we hear interiorly, when we look out the window at certain moments of our life.

The old lady stopped for a moment. During this brief break, she exchanged hands with her bags. One might say that nothing has really changed; she's still carrying the same bags with the same weight. If she wanted to get where she was going, there really was not much more she could do. Yet in that moment, her hands got a rest, their load was fleetingly lightened, they reestablished their balance. It's true that in reality, nothing has changed, and yet as she resumes her journey, everything is different.

How to speak of this meaningful moment? I suggest "a moment of changing hands." Obviously, it is not her *hands* that change; the left hand does not become the right hand. But I like this kind of play (and wisdom) that language pushes us to. Obviously, what changes is what each of her hands holds. Language, after all, does not describe what is visible in an exhaustive way, otherwise we'd never be able to describe anything. When one changes hands while carrying a burden in them, we give our tired hands the opportunity to rest, restore balance, and then move ahead anew. The tired hands remain the same and, at the same time, they are different. Perhaps we place little value on such a "moment of changing hands," but it is thanks to this that the old lady, though she feels her strength failing, manages to bring home what she needs.

Human omnipotence is an illusion that ends up crumbling. Truth be told, there is no one who does not experience vulnerability. There is no one who doesn't feel, at one time or another, that the burdens of life are too heavy to go on, that some challenges are achievable and others are impossible, that a moment for rest and restoration is needed. Even if, constrained by necessity or absorbed by pleasure, we extend our journey disproportionately, there is a moment when we need to raise our heads, stand up, stretch our legs, and take a break, a pause, however small, to breathe fresh air. This becomes a requirement if we are to move forward with renewed vitality.

The French art historian Henri Focillon, in his beautiful work *In Praise of Hands*, recalled nearly a century ago that there are dimensions of life that we can only know through our hands. He reflected on the meaning of the fingers and the concavity of the hands, recognizing their fragility and firmness. He wrote,

> Those things that weigh an unperceivable weight or beat the warm beating of life: those things with a crust, a dress, a coat, or even the stone, broken, smoothed by water or whose texture has remained intact, these are all a job for the hand, because it is the goal of an experience that sight and mind cannot capture by themselves.[5]

Our eyes slide on the surface of the universe, but nothing gives us the measure of reality more than the contact our feet and our hands make with the world. When was the last time we switched hands with our bags?

TOUCHED BY MERCY

If we never set ourselves free to truly desire to be born from above, in the way that Jesus spoke to Nicodemus (John 3:1–21), we will always be "elderly." Even if times are new, we will continue to age. Let's be realistic: adulthood is a cemetery of disappointments, losses, resentments, and missed opportunities. Doesn't all of this have to do with our inability to be like the birds of the air or the lilies of the fields, creating prisons for ourselves where we hold captive our very selves, like birds in a cage? We want to go further, but we always stumble on the same stones: we are not reconciled. This leaves us constantly with a lack of confidence in life. The purification of memory is not only a journey into the past. It consists in letting the mystery of Mercy touch us, to say a total yes to the present moment that we are living.

In one of his most memorable poems, "The Butterfly," Tonino Guerra tells of the day he was released from the concentration camp and realized that his freedom was more than exterior:

> Happy, truly happy
> I have been many times in my life,
> but never so much as when,
> after I was released in Germany,
> I started looking at a butterfly
> without wanting to eat it.[6]

WHEN WE DON'T LET OURSELVES BE TOUCHED

Sometimes when we allow nothing and no one to touch us, the difficulty is in us. Our basic problem is an unwillingness to love, to love ourselves, our face, our body, our age, our culture, what we have or don't have, what we know or don't know. We don't like ourselves, and we don't love ourselves. We are unhappy. We sometimes disguise this emptiness with a pride and a self-sufficiency that only hide (though poorly) our deep fragility. Learning to love oneself is the task of a lifetime. It's something that never ends. We are constantly discovering what it means.

When we love ourselves, we also know how to love others. We learn to pay attention to others and to serve others. But even that is not always love. We sometimes give a lot, but we cannot give ourselves. Often, what we take for love is, in fact, a form of power over others, a way of having them in hand, controlling them, manipulating them, obtaining their admiration. True love is about offering our love to others without worrying about what they are going to do with it.

Meister Eckhart wrote, "If you love yourself, you love all [people] as yourself. As long as you love one single person less than yourself, you have never really loved yourself."[7]

THE TOUCH THAT HEALS

In the field of medical care, awareness has grown that touching the sick—not just with the clinical contact demanded by treatment, but with human touches—can be a significant factor in the therapeutic process. When a patient is touched in an appropriate and nonintrusive way, her or his humanity, self-esteem, and confidence are stimulated, and these facilitate recovery. A health-care professional should be aware that sometimes a simple touch helps reduce discomfort, soothes restless feelings, and conveys comfort that no device or medication can give.

WE HAVE TO LEARN

Cicely Saunders, the doctor who founded the first palliative care unit, wrote, "We have to learn." We must learn to manage and reduce pain, but not only with pills—also with the heart, physical presence, silent gestures, and respect, with the help of the courage of those who are sick. Those who are sick don't want or need our indulgence. We must learn to embrace fragility, that of others and our own, too; to help people treasure memories, nurture hope, and give meaning to what remains of life, however tiny and fragile it may be. We must learn to be supportive, to prize technical efficiency but also compassion. We must recognize the value of a smile, even an imperfect one, at difficult moments. Endings bring so many beginnings.

For example, one of my most cherished memories comes from my father's last hospital stay. I walked hand in hand with my dad day after day, slowly, through the wide hallway of the hospital. Through my hand, I transmitted to him all the strength that I could, but his hand was larger than mine. It will always be so, I know it.

WHAT IS AN EMBRACE?

What is an embrace? It is quite possible that one of the first hugs we gave someone was only to hang on so as not to fall. However, little by little, during a patient process during which the bodies learn about themselves (and about love), the embrace ceases to be something that you give me or that I give you. It arises as a new thing, a thing that did not yet exist in the world and that we create together.

2

YEARNING FOR INFINITE FLAVOR

THE FLAVOR OF HOME

Here is a story told by the Spanish writer José Luis Sampedro in his novel *La sonrisa etrusca* (The Etruscan Smile). An old peasant from Calabria, a rural region in southern Italy, went to stay in Milan with his son and daughter-in-law, while he was in the city for some medical appointments. The difference between the man's life in the countryside and his son's life in the city could not have been greater. The old man felt disoriented. He couldn't believe the way his son, a lawyer, lived—the exhausting rhythm, the building in which the neighbors didn't know each other, the tasteless food. One evening when his son's wife was away on a trip, before his son got home from work, the old man prepared a surprise for dinner. When they sat down at the table together, the dishes were ready, properly covered to stay warm. Before unveiling the meal, the father asked his son whether he could identify the food by its smell. "A familiar and yet unclassifiable smell, ancient and penetrating. That smell…." It was *migas*, a traditional dish of Southern Europe. Fantastic country *migas*, seasoned with basil and other herbs that the old man had found by their aroma in a little grocery store amidst the turbulence of the big city. As the son ate, a door in his memory slowly opened. His mind was filled with shepherds and chestnuts, campfires and songs, childhood foods and motherly hands. Suddenly, the father began to say a few sentences in the Calabrian dialect, and then the son joined him. These were the happiest hours they spent together during the father's visit. At the end of dinner, when it was time to wish each other a good night, they exchanged a hug, a strong embrace that expressed their renewed emotional bond.

This story shows how the flavor of familiar and local dishes offers the ultimate possibility of a return to one's origins, when all other connections are lost. It is common, for example, for immigrants to adopt the diet of their host country on a daily basis; but on certain occasions—especially the most significant ones, like a birthday or a party—only the flavor of home provides the taste of joy.

THE BIBLE IN FLAVORS

"I went to the angel and told him to give me the little scroll; and he said to me, 'Take it, and eat'" (Rev 10:9). This passage from the Book of Revelation is a good illustration of our relationship to the sacred text. The Bible introduces a link between reading and eating not limited to metaphor. The Bible is eaten. It is fragrant, abundant like the celestial banquet, intimate like the family table, sweet to the palate. We read in its pages of copious secular banquets and sacred meals, ascetic deserts and the delights of the palate, rare game and abundant pastures, frugal foods of the road and banquets long awaited. It is a collection not just of words, but of flavors.

If we pay attention to the many aspects of food, eating, and dietary prescriptions in the Bible, we can go so far as to say that it offers an authentic theology of food and that the sacred Judeo-Christian text is a splendid catalogue of recipes. In fact, we can understand biblical revelation more deeply through eating. Reading it constitutes a fascinating initiation into flavors: the milk and honey, roasted grain, unleavened bread, the Passover meal.

THE BREAD OF EVERY PLEASURE

Manna is the food God brought down from the sky (it fell from the sky like morning dew) so his people could survive the long desert crossing. The first gastronomic description of manna, in Exodus 16, is very generic: it is simply presented as "bread." Further on, the Book of Numbers gives us more detailed information:

> The manna was like coriander seed, and its color was like the color of gum resin. The people went around and gathered it, ground it in mills or beat it in mortars, then boiled it in pots and made cakes of it; and the taste of it was like the taste of cakes baked with oil. (Num 11:7–8)

Other descriptions of this food appear elsewhere in the Bible. The summit of this analogical construction is probably this passage from the Book of Wisdom: "You gave your people food of angels, / and without their toil you supplied them from heaven with bread ready to eat, / providing every pleasure and suited to every taste" (Wis 16:20). The passage goes on to explain the wonder that made this modest manna a bread of "every pleasure": "For your sustenance manifested your sweetness toward your children; / and the bread, ministering to the desire of the one who took it, / was changed to suit everyone's liking" (v. 21). As though to express the excellence of God's gift, all flavors are attributed to it.

Taste, then, is related to God's love, and to love in general. God can be tasted. God is flavor.

TASTING GOD

Tasting God! This is what the Psalter offers us and not by chance, because the psalms express faith in the first person singular. The psalms are not about concepts; they are poetry and prayer. Their words are about the body and time—the surprise, pain, and delight of being human. Everyday human experience is the starting point for a relationship with God, a relationship that is rarely linear, never predictable or repetitive. Like the original authors of the psalms, the believer who appropriates them as her own does not separate faith from emotions. When it is time to dance, she dances; when it is time to bless, she blesses; and when it comes to crying out in the darkest night, that cry is one of vibrant truth. Our prayer must reflect the fire of life. No wonder, then, that among the passages in the Bible that refer to taste and flavor, the psalms occupy such a special place.

In Psalm 27, the Psalmist prays,

> One thing I asked of the LORD,
>   that will I seek after:
> to live in the house of the LORD
>   all the days of my life,
> to behold [or some translations say: savor] the beauty of
>   the LORD,
>   and to inquire in his temple. (v. 4)

How do we savor? By choosing not to just devour everything; by allowing an interior slowness to hold sway; by contemplating with our taste buds, with our body; by being attentive, observing, allowing ourselves to be surprised, and letting the epiphany emerge.

Taste is a form of intimacy that requires deep contact. Unlike the things that remain external to us and that we can appreciate, evaluate, and distinguish, taste always implies a more complete relationship. We needn't rush. The finer the meal on the palate, the more we eat it in small bites, to make the experience last. In the smallest portion, we perceive the maximum flavor; in this tiny crumb, we enjoy intense sweetness. It's not just about filling our stomach or satisfying our hunger.

Psalm 34 then strikes us. Again, we are caught between a liturgical hymn of praise for an assembly and an autobiographical confession. This is also revealed in the use of "I" and "you" in the text. The starting point is a personal experience, as we can see from the first lines:

> My soul makes its boast in the LORD;
>   let the humble hear and be glad.
> O magnify the LORD with me,
>   and let us exalt his name together.
>
> I sought the LORD, and he answered me,
>   and delivered me from all my fears. (vv. 1–4)

This is an experience of God, based not on an abstraction, but on a living, concrete relationship. The search has received a response; a deliverance "from all my fears" has occurred. For this reason, the extraordinary challenge offered by the Psalmist in verse 8 is not rash. He knows in whom he has put his trust, and firmly anchored, he says, "O taste and see that the LORD is good; / happy are those who take refuge in him." Why taste? Taste awakens us, illuminates us, and spreads within us until it becomes a part of us.

In the New Testament, 1 Peter is a homiletic rereading of this theology of tasting God that we find in the psalms. In what is clearly a paraphrase of the psalm, Peter tells us, "Like newborn infants, long for the pure, spiritual milk, so that by it you may grow into salvation—if indeed you have tasted that the Lord is good" (1 Pet 2:2–3).

THE FLAVOR WE BECOME

Jesus speaks of flavor, too. Matthew and Luke report this teaching in a similar way: "You are the salt of the earth; but if salt has lost

its taste, how can its saltiness be restored? It is no longer good for anything, but is thrown out and trampled under foot" (Matt 5:13; cf. Luke
14:34–35). However, Mark's version includes a curious alteration: "Salt
is good; but if the salt has lost its saltiness, how can you season it? Have
salt in yourselves, and be at peace with one another" (Mark 9:50).

What is new in Mark is this final phrase: "Have salt in yourselves." Flavor is not something that we carry outwardly; it is a way
of being, something we become. What Jesus wants is that we live
lives that have flavor, not lives of bland broth. Jesus rejects being
neutral; he calls us to flavor and to the risk of living. Indifference
about life has no place in following him.

A NEW TABLE PROTOCOL

The bone of contention that many had about Jesus was not
simply that he ate and drank. Indeed, the religious authorities of the
time severely criticized the asceticism of certain movements. The
problem was that Jesus was not careful enough about the *kinds* of
people he ate *with*. That is, he relativized the rules of ritual purity
and made meals occasions for an encounter beyond the limits established by the law. By accepting the invitation of sinners to sit with
them at table, Jesus was going against the powerful code of purity on
which socioreligious cohesion was based. Furthermore, the meal was
the means he chose to offer an unprecedented experience of God. In
the universalist line of the messianic banquet, which the prophets
of Israel had said would mark the world to come, Jesus rejected a
religion taken hostage by moral and social legalism, and he made
God's mercy accessible. For this reason, he ignored the prohibitions
and turned the meal protocol upside down.

This strategy of Jesus is already clear in the first meal he shares
with sinners (Luke 5:29–32). A tax collector named Levi, whom Jesus
has called to be one of his disciples, hosts a banquet for Jesus at his home.
This fact does not go unnoticed by the authorities, and this question

arises: "Why do you eat and drink with tax collectors and sinners?" (v. 30). Jesus's response reveals the originality of his ministry. He doesn't focus on the abolition of norms as such; rather, he refers to the emergence of a higher meaning, which he now represents: "Those who are well have no need of a physician, but those who are sick; I have come to call not the righteous but sinners to repentance" (vv. 31–32).

The fact that Jesus sits at table with sinners explains the meaning of his mission: to proclaim God's forgiveness and make it concrete. There is no doubt that the experience of God's mercy is, in a way, in continuity with the biblical tradition that preceded it; but this insistence, prefigured in the meal, of God's unconditional welcome is a rejection of the religious apparatus that was then in place. It is not so much that sinners convert to obtain mercy and forgiveness; rather, sinners are *sought* after by Mercy and are converted. The path proposed by Jesus directly opposes the theology taught by the temple authorities. In the peculiar hermeneutics of this Mediterranean peasant, the revelation of the kingdom of God is introduced in a disconcerting way: by the people who are gathered around a table. Meals are performative acts for Jesus; there he reveals his mission by gathering around the same table those who cannot be together, by preparing an egalitarian meal for the disparate multitude.

Jesus's opponents perceived his habit of eating at the table of sinners as an anarchic and provocative gesture, but those who followed him saw this as an expression and confirmation that in him the kingdom of God had arrived and that the salvation of all was a reality made possible. By eating with sinners, Jesus embodied the kingdom that he proclaimed. It is not surprising that this is perceived as a fundamental messianic act.

When Jesus sent his disciples, he charged them with a similar mission. He told them not to have a purse or a bag. Cynical,[1] itinerant preachers begged for food and needed a satchel to carry what they were given. In Jewish tradition, such a satchel was also used to carry the payment one received for teaching. The disciples of Jesus, however, shared the gospel proclamation with the people they encountered, entering their homes and sitting at their tables. The table is a kind of symbolic border that testifies to the unexpected meeting of diverse people and effectively makes communion possible. The giving of alms is an approach, but it does not really break down borders. The common table, on the contrary, establishes reciprocal relationships. For this reason, the codes of honor and the rules of purity—moral purity, ritual purity, ethnic purity—that were so important in structuring Mediterranean societies were threatened by collapse with the appearance of Christian communities that established egalitarian and fraternal bonds between people of unequal conditions or who did not know each other.

THE FLAVOR OF WHAT FEEDS US

One of the last things Jesus said to his apostles was, "I have eagerly desired to eat this Passover with you before I suffer" (Luke 22:15). It is interesting to note his use of the verb *desire*, because it directly connects the meal with desire.

A sentence from the Talmud says, "Before a person eats and drinks, he has two hearts, but after eating and drinking he has only one heart."[2] Before we eat, we are divided, distracted by various desires. After eating, a person redefines himself, finds himself, trusts. The spiritual journey means being present to oneself, to one's soul, to one's place. For this reason, no one will find her soul if she also does not find the meaning and the flavor of what nourishes her.

SOMETIMES BANQUETS ARE ONLY WORDS

I will never forget how one of the most extraordinary meals I have ever tasted was made up of words. It was offered by the poet

Tonino Guerra, in an account of a group of Italian resistance fighters held in a German concentration camp during World War II. Christmas Day had arrived and with it always the same ration of misery. To console themselves, everyone began to talk about what they ate at home on Christmas Day: *tagliatella al ragu, ravioli bolognese*, veal with wine sauce and polenta, and so on. At that point, someone—the story doesn't say who it is, but it was probably Guerra himself—had an idea: they should prepare a meal together.

"We can make a feast with words!" he said.

"And how is it possible?" his fellow prisoners asked.

Guerra then began to speak faster, giving instructions to those around him: "You heat the water. You go get an onion. Quick, quick, fry it in the pan. You watch the fire. Add four tablespoons of oil. You bring the ground beef. A glass of white wine, where's the white wine? Magnificent! Do you already smell the aroma? Bring salt and pepper. Almost done. Drain it quickly. You bring the tomato sauce to add it. I'll sprinkle it with a cloud of Parmesan and…here we are! (He claps his hands.) Quickly, quickly, each of you bring your plate."

The men opened their hands to receive their plates and made confident gestures as though they were eating, slowly savoring the invisible wonder. When the last of them was served, the first asked, "Can I have seconds?"

"HAVE A GOOD SUNDAY AND A GOOD LUNCH!"

Buona domenica e buon pranzo!—"Have a good Sunday and a good lunch!" Pope Francis often uses this line when he says goodbye to the faithful who gather in St. Peter's Square every Sunday for the midday recitation of the Angelus. We should notice how unusual this is. Recent popes have concluded with a blessing or a smile. We remember John Paul II in that window during the last months of his life, when some commentators wondered aloud whether revealing so much suffering so directly was not excessive, or Benedict XVI's final Angelus before his abdication. For those who wanted to see it, everything was there. The form their communication took was neither better nor worse; it was simply different. But what touches so many people about Pope Francis's style is his rare capacity to be close, familiar, to express concrete attention toward others.

Translated by Pope Francis, pastoral ministry ceases to be an abstract science, made up of graphics and flowcharts. It doesn't follow categorizations or manuals. It is Evangelical, intuitive, and inclusive. It becomes an art that the heart knows (and recognizes). It is a relationship of trust that accepts the permanent need to question itself. It goes beyond the formal framework where, unfortunately, evangelization often stops.

When Jesus sent his disciples out, he told them to go into people's homes, sit at their tables, and eat and drink what they offered (see Luke 10:3–7). In this communion of table and destiny is lived one of the most surprising journeys that one can make, whatever the time or the civilization: to transcend the space that separates us from others, overcome the obstacles that separate the world between strangers and family. When we hear Pope Francis wishing us "a good Sunday and a good lunch," it is not just a formal and polite way to conclude. It's more than that. Much more.

WHEN NOT EATING IS A PRAYER

Only an insipid Christianity would dare to suggest that fasting is inappropriate or that fasting from food could be replaced by some other practice, like depriving oneself of some other good thing or avoiding an unnecessary expense. Fasting teaches us deeply, in a unique way, about what nourishes us and about the somnambulant voracity in which we live. Indeed, as the Portuguese priest José Augusto Mourão said, "There is in us a desire to be, to live, that no food in the world can fulfill. What we desire is not so much the things that we think we need, but what underlies it all: the gift of life." This is precisely what fasting is about.

In its biblical and Christian conception, fasting is not a simple detoxification from the overconsumption in which we are immersed, but a means, both symbolic and real, to express that *the real food* of our life is other, is elsewhere. Thus, we are called to consider fasting as an occasion when we can pay attention again to the spiritual in an authentic way—and this through conversion. It is to the extent that the believer deepens the unwavering love of God that he or she can accept the risk and the demand for such a vital compromise.

In its political symbolism (which it obviously has, let's not forget), fasting also openly challenges a culture that believes it finds happiness in consumption, that promotes this quest for happiness in an egocentric and primary way. Fasting is a rejection of the bubbling desires rooted in the self that each of us carries. The Christian life is an economy of resistance and combat. Fasting must become an active commitment to transform the oppressive structures of a world that, for example, in its present form, encourages the greedy to plunder the planet's resources.

Fasting, therefore, only finds its legitimacy when it brings us closer to others, places our action in a community perspective, and strengthens our relationships. It is to the extent that the believer firmly anchors her practice in relationships that she will be able to understand the true meaning of fasting: the renouncement of the self-centered attitude of the different types of consumption with a view to *sobriety, sharing, solidarity*, and *self-giving*. Fasting should inspire a new quality and a new style of relationship, moving us away from both predatory practices whose incentives we are subjected to every day and from the indifference caused by the obsessive pursuit of individual profit.

The Portuguese monk Carlos Maria Antunes writes in his aptly titled book *So o pobre se faz pao* (Only the Poor Make Bread),

> Fasting makes us vulnerable. It confronts us with our nakedness, frees us from the tyranny of masks, and exposes us to the radical poverty that inhabits every human being. It tells us that we are hungry for more than bread and that our deepest desire is always the desire for the other. By expanding our interior space, it is transformed into a singular form of hospitality, which allows the reception of oneself and the other in its originality and its purest truth.

IN PRAISE OF FRUGALITY

On the topic of frugality, perhaps it is important to start by stating what it is *not*. The first necessary distinction is this: frugality must not be confused with poverty. While one might develop a whole series of reasons behind poverty (social, financial, personal), the obvious always ends up emerging: poverty is not the result of free choice. Frugality is.

We also must avoid comparing frugality to avarice, or stinginess. People typically become stingy in reaction to psychological wounds and fears. Stinginess, as we know, is a kind of lonely, sad, and hopeless obsession.

Frugality is also more than a decision to save money. There are good reasons for putting money aside. The future is not assured, and we can provide for it in the present. So we cut expenses and avoid the frenzy to consume everything we think we want in order to better face the uncertainties of the future. It is true that frugality also has the effect of producing savings, but this is merely one of its side effects.

So what is frugality? It's the choice for what is small, to live in a small way, by deriving maximum meaning from it. Abundance is a confused and undifferentiated state, without distinctions, where everything is mixed together—what is needed and what is unnecessary, what is new and what is repeated, what is unique and what is banal, what we consume and the happiness we think it will bring. Frugality breaks away, distances itself, acquires a critical conscience, refuses to give up its freedom. Frugality is a style. Henry David Thoreau's comment about frugality is particularly enlightening: "A man is rich in proportion to the number of things which he can afford to let alone."[3]

In the Gospel of Luke, we find a crucial sentence of Jesus that, at first sight, seems enigmatic, but which can become for us a road map. To the busy hostess Martha, Jesus said, "Martha, Martha, you are worried and distracted by many things; there is need of only one thing" (Luke 10:41–42). This comment is enigmatic, because Jesus does not quite say clearly what the one thing needed actually *is*. It is a road map when we understand that only we can solve the enigma and that the answer may vary throughout our lives.

We can travel through our lives with a small suitcase or a large one. The size of the suitcase does not matter. Whether it's full because it's small or because we have filled a large one with many things, we will have to take some things out of it if we want to be able to put new things in. We then spend our life doing this: accumulating, emptying, accumulating, emptying. With frugality, the size of the suitcase is unimportant. The frugal traveler is one who has made the decision in advance to carry just the essentials, always leaving space available in the suitcase.

WHO GIVES A DRINK TO WHOM?

In a well-known story in the Gospel of John (4:5–42), Jesus meets a Samaritan woman and makes an extraordinary request:

"Give me a drink." What the Lord is asking is this: "Give me a drink. That is, give me what you have and what you don't have, give me what you carry and what you've lost, give me what you are." This request puts us before the surprise of love. Though he bore a divine nature, as St. Paul reminds us, Jesus did not claim his right to be treated as God (see Phil 2:6–11). Offering us the opportunity to make our fragile and human contribution, the Lord tells us, "Give me a drink." This is remarkable because it turns our expectations upside down. We know all about what it means to be thirsty. We know hunger. Necessity punctures our precarious existence. Now suddenly Jesus comes and says, "No, you're the one who will give me a drink." He restores the possibility of a covenant by the most surprising of revelations.

The Samaritan woman felt the surprise and the difficulty of this request. She tried to escape from Jesus, asking how he, a Jew, could ask her for a drink, but Jesus did not shy away from the answer: "If you knew the gift of God, and who it is that is saying to you, 'Give me a drink,' you would have asked him" (v. 10). We are very caught up in our resistances, our fears, our hesitations, as if our hindrances carry more weight than the hospitality to which Jesus calls us. We find so many excuses, good or bad, for not abandoning ourselves to love. Like the Samaritan woman, we look at life and ask ourselves, "Lord, how are you going to draw water from this well?" Basically, we lack confidence in the power of God. The real problem for most of us is not doubting that God is the Lord of history; it's doubting that God is the Lord of *our* history. It is not doubting that God created the world; that we can probably accept easily. The thorniest difficulty is to believe with all our strength that the Lord can re-create our interior world, reconfigure our existence. Like the Samaritan woman, we say to God, "You have no bucket, and the well is deep" (v. 11).

WHAT BECOMES OF OUR DESIRE?

Certain questions always await our response. We can avoid them, try to circumvent them, or evade the subject for a long time. But deep down, we know that this game of hide-and-seek has a price. To withdraw from it is to withdraw from ourselves and to miss the call of life. One of these questions, in its most incisive and personal form, can be formulated like this: *What is my desire?* What is my deep desire, one that does not depend on any possession or necessity, that does not refer to an object, but to the very meaning of life? *What is my desire?* What is the desire that has nothing to do with the daily impulses that push us to consume, but that has rather to do with the broad horizon of accomplishment, of the realization of myself as a unique and inimitable person, the transfiguration of who I am, my exterior and interior self (both are so vital), my silence, my language?

Consumer society pretends that everyone can be satisfied by having enough of what it offers; it misleadingly identifies happiness with satiation. Satisfied, sated, filled, tamed—our needs fulfilled by the festival of consumption (at least we think so). But the satiety that is obtained through consumption is a prison of desire, reduced to an impulse to be satisfied immediately. True desire, meanwhile, is experienced as an emptiness, a dissatisfaction that becomes a dynamic and motivating principle. This desire is literally insatiable because it yearns for what cannot be possessed: the meaning of life. From this perspective, desire is not something that is satisfied, but that deepens.

Because of all this, we cannot ask ourselves "What is my desire?" without taking the first step of a journey that begins only when we dare to enter into ourselves, to understand the person who looks back at us from the mirror. As the French psychoanalyst Françoise Dolto says, when this moment arrives, "when a human being feels a desire strong enough to assume all the risks of his being, he is ready to honor the life he has been given."

What happens then? It is up to us to question, to reflect, to hesitate, to reflect on our experience, to look differently at various moments. Perhaps we will understand what Merleau-Ponty meant when he said, "Loneliness and communication are not alternatives to choose from, but two aspects of the same phenomenon." Perhaps, for the first time, we will venture out of the routine, out of the sleepy and supposedly comfortable pattern in which we lock up our lives.

In doing so, it will be particularly difficult to encounter repressed suffering and to embrace the pain caused by recognizing it. At unsuspected depths there is pain that we'd long forgotten, but which conditions everything about us, even in our public lives. Identifying and managing this pain is the condition for becoming who we are and for being able to understand the pain of others, by touching our truth and theirs. Accepting ourselves, with all our shortcomings and vulnerabilities, is a critical and sometimes heartbreaking stage, but it opens us to the possibility of transformation and fruitfulness. It opens us to the formulation of desire, and let's not forget, accepted vulnerability often becomes a window through which the unexpected transparency of grace enters.

The human person, each of us, is *homo desirans*, but we must often ask ourselves what we have done with our desire.

IN THE DESERT, A SPRING

How shall we describe the situation we're in? We place bets based on what we think is a good grasp of our circumstances, without realizing that we only understand small pieces and never the whole thing, never the fullness we want. It seems to us that our hearts are breaking, our enthusiasm is cooling, our steps are getting heavier. We drink from so many fountains, but our thirst always comes back. We experience temporary satiation and not having a transparent, enlightened heart. We know what it is to search, to knock on different doors insistently, and to continue to wait for an answer. Sometimes we feel that even if we could drink all the water in the world, our thirst would not be quenched. Then we repeat the beautiful and sad refrain that the great Swedish writer Stig Sagermann offers in one of his books: "Our need for consolation is impossible to satisfy."

But Jesus knows this. He knows our tragedy of always being thirsty, and he tells us, "Everyone who drinks of this water will be thirsty again, but those who drink of the water that I will give them will never be thirsty. The water that I will give will become in them a spring of water gushing up to eternal life" (John 4:13–14).

Look at what Jesus is offering us: that he will put a spring in our hearts and that we discover within us the source of divine life. Only then will we no longer thirst, our anxiety will heal, our pain will subside, our problems will keep their proper proportions. It's not just about sewing a patch on a torn life, because repairing old fabric is useless. On the contrary, it is about discovering that in the very heart of *the desert that I am*, God puts a spring of *living water*, and that changes everything.

SLOWLY SO WE CAN TASTE

When we're in a hurry, we can't taste. We need to rediscover the art of going slowly. Our lifestyles seem irreparably stressed by a pressure that we do not control. There's no time to lose; we want to reach our goals as quickly as possible. Processes wear us down, questions delay us, and feelings are a pure waste of energy. We are told that only results matter. Only results! At this rate, our rhythms of activity become ruthlessly unnatural. Every new activity seems more engaging and demands to take precedence over everything else. Our schedules eat away our private lives. We should, however, think more carefully about what we lose, what we leave in the background, submerged or muted, what we no longer know when we allow acceleration to condition us this way.

In a magnificent novel called *Slowness*, Milan Kundera wrote,

> There is a secret bond between slowness and memory, between speed and forgetting. A man is walking down the street. At a certain moment, he tries to recall something, but the recollection escapes him. Automatically, he slows down. Meanwhile, a person who wants to forget a disagreeable incident he has just lived through starts unconsciously to speed up his pace, as if he were trying to distance himself from a thing still too close to him in time.
>
> In existential mathematics that experience takes the form of two basic equations: The degree of slowness is directly proportional to the intensity of memory; the degree of speed is directly proportional to the intensity of forgetting.[4]

Hurrying gives us the impression that an experience is imaginary. Contrary to what it seems, its ally is not memory but forgetfulness. Everything ends at the same speed as it begins.

We need to reconsider our relationship with time, to do things more carefully, in smaller steps. This cannot happen without an interior calm. Precisely because the urgency to make decisions is enormous, we need a slowness that protects us from doing it mechanically, from blindly compulsive moves, from repetitive and banal speech.

This reminds me of a funny story I heard from the Portuguese artist Lourdes de Castro. On certain days, when the phone kept ringing and deadlines got shorter and everything suddenly demanded more speed than she could give, she and her husband Manuel Zimbro began to walk through their house with theatrical slowness. Breaking out of the vicious circle of urgency, they laughed, saved time, and stepped back, looking for other ways to respond;

they felt closer to each other and renewed. It is up to each of us to find the modalities of slowness that suit us best.

Even if slowness has lost almost all consideration in our modern Western societies, it remains an antidote against normalizing the expectations for constant speed. Slowness is an attempt to flee from what is "square," that is, it dares to transcend what is solely functional and useful. It often chooses to live with silence. It notices small changes in meaning, nuances of light, changes in flavor.

WE ARE THE LAND OF WATER, AND YET…

Here's a story.

Once upon a time there was the land of wells. One might think that a country like that must be pretty, green, a haven in which the birds come to fill themselves up and perform their dancing flights in the open air; the land of wells is surely a well-populated, attractive land, full of life. But think again: it was a devastated desert. Over time, the water at the bottom of the wells had begun to dry up. Almost imperceptibly, they became not sources of water but holes full of rubble. All the things that had accumulated in them ended up stifling their purpose and their beauty. As the water was relegated to the very bottom, the desert began to expand around them. With the desert came loneliness, the weight of a life where everything ends up turning against it. One day, however, a well said no. This well had heard in the depths of itself the rhythm of a forgotten music that was in it but silenced for so long. It then began to clear away its detritus to find what filled it with curiosity. While searching, its passion grew. After many years, it finally approached a treasure that one could neither buy nor sell. It was a reality deep inside. It was water. Because it was emptied, the water could again flow and spread. Around this well, life flourished, and then the other wells began to follow its example. Because all the water came from a vigorous spring, this immense desert was able to become green again.

We are the land of living water. Despite that, we are too often more like deserts. We are more like heaps of rubble than places where the fountain of eternity finds its home and expression. Suddenly, we feel that life is running out, that everything we see is coming to an end, that our hope only exists in the ephemeral, in the instant that vanishes like smoke. For this reason, there is a fundamental spiritual realism that tells us: no interior journey can be made if we do not have the courage to empty ourselves, to cast out what clutters or distracts us, in order to be able to welcome the limpid flavor of this ignored but ultimately accessible fountain deep inside of us.

THE LONELINESS THAT LEADS TO THE SPRING

Spiritual life is not a theory or an abstraction. It is not a virtual moment or a projection of our imagination. It's an experience, an attentiveness, an immersion. We know that there is a dark and heavy loneliness that can arise when we look at life and think that we have never been loved. This loneliness is terrible and yet so common. But there is another kind of loneliness, a luminous solitude where words fail us because we are confronted with an overflowing, living, abiding presence.

Guilt or self-flagellation do not convert our hearts. What transforms us is the experience of love, an inordinately passionate love, like the love that God has for the person that we are. It is through contact with this love that we change. For this reason, the only solitude in which we can trust is that which leads us very slowly toward a source.

There is a passage from Saint-Exupéry's *The Little Prince* that I return to often:

"Good morning," said the little prince.

"Good morning," said the merchant.

This was a merchant who sold pills that had been invented to quench thirst. You need only swallow one pill a week, and you would feel no need of anything to drink.

"Why are you selling those?" asked the little prince.

"Because they save a tremendous amount of time," said the merchant. "Computations have been made by experts. With these pills, you save fifty-three minutes in every week."

"And what do I do with those fifty-three minutes?"

"Anything you like…"

"As for me," said the little prince to himself, "if I had fifty-three minutes to spend as I liked, I should walk at my leisure toward a spring of fresh water."[5]

UNDERSTANDING AND SAVORING

In the introduction to his *Spiritual Exercises*, St. Ignatius explained, "What fills and satisfies the soul consists not in knowing much, but in our understanding the realities profoundly and in savoring them interiorly."[6] These two verbs—*understanding* and *savoring*—sum up well the experience of God that St. Ignatius offers us.

Taste—savoring—is a very particular mode of knowledge because it is an awareness of our interior response to an external stimulus that enters us. Taste is about the presence of that outside thing in us. Through taste, we internalize what is around us or make decisions about whether to: enjoy the pleasure of it, receive it cautiously, avoid it. It is important not to ignore these resonances, because to ignore them is to avoid understanding oneself. Taste is a crucial element in all mystical spirituality.

TIME TO TASTE

With experience, we can understand that the most important thing is not to decide whether life is, all things considered, beautiful or tragic, a trivial passion or a sublime enterprise. We can welcome it as all these things, apparently so different and contradictory. Life is, mysteriously, a combination of truth and pain, joy and fatigue, love and loneliness. If we know how to welcome, with all our inner strength, these different facets, they will become many possible paths to explore, but we later learn that this is not even the most important thing. The most important thing is to know, with the absolute certainty that comes from the bottom of our soul, whether we are ready to love life as it comes.

We come to understand that talking about air as the poet Tonino Guerra does is not a silly fantasy, but a concrete way of looking at life:

> Air is that light thing,
> that is around your head
> and becomes clearer when you laugh.[7]

Simone Weil's conviction that "attention is prayer"[8] calls us to live in the "now," because if we do not have the prudence and the generosity to keep our eyes wide open to the present, what can the future teach us? Life has a simplicity that we need to rediscover, by stripping ourselves of what hinders us, by launching ourselves again into its obstinate flow. We are often deprived of life, separated from it by a wall of words, anxiety, and unrealistic expectations. We must break through this wall to truly encounter life.

We therefore must choose between an illusory love of life, which constantly makes us postpone it, and a real, even wounded, love that allows us to accept life as it is; between loving life for what we expect to get from it and loving it unconditionally for what it is, often in complete helplessness, loss, and deficiency. To condition the joy of living upon a dreamed happiness is already to lose it because—we needn't be afraid to say it out loud—life is disappointing. With the deep spiritual clarity that sometimes decidedly unspiritual people attain, Oscar Wilde has one of his characters say, "In this world there are only two tragedies. One is not getting what one wants, and the other is getting it."[9]

We must let go of our narcissistic attachment to an idealized life and to accept life as it comes, without lies or illusions, which requires of us a much richer and more difficult love. It is to a large extent a work of mourning, a path of purification, without giving up the complexity of its existence, but accepting that it cannot be fully explained. Life is what remains despite everything: an existence without tinsel, small, unclear, but more precious than anything. Wisdom is life itself: the reality of everyday life, approaching it not as in a truce, but a pact, known and accepted in its fascinating and painful entirety.

"When does the hour of happiness come?" we ask ourselves. It happens in the moments of grace when we expect nothing. As the seventeenth-century German mystic Angelus Silesius teaches us:

> The rose is without why
> She blooms because she blooms
> She pays herself no heed
> asks not if one can see her.[10]

THE UNIQUE FLAVOR

One of the most beautiful poems—and one of the most extraordinary prayers—that I know about flavor is by Portuguese poet António Ramos Rosa. The poem *La saveur unique* (The Unique Flavor) was published in a collection in 1960. It has an interesting literary history, because the volume in which it appears, entitled *Voz inicial* (First Voice),[11] marks a new stage in Ramos Rosa's poetry, which had until this point been centered especially on the denunciation of sociopolitical constraints and their impact on individual conscience. It is not that Ramos Rosa's social concern is now absent, but it is integrated into a broader questioning of the historical and spiritual meaning of the human adventure. Here, the sense of taste, around which this poetic text is built, is emblematic, because it puts us in a zone of contact between the here and the now, between what is close and beyond them, close and beyond us. This magnificent poem concludes with these lines:

> O flavor of the dark, of the breast, of the thickness of
>   the night,
> O deep sleep of the roots,
> O thou, water drunk from the earth, O dream of life,
> O rustling of animals, of everything and nothing, in the
>   same obscure silence,
> O land near me, O great and foreign land,
> O lost proximity, O lost distance,
> O huge sound of seashells,
> O tranquil gardens, O flavor of exhaustion,
> O flavor that precedes me,
> O time when I did not know, but when everything in
>   me knew
> O night, O thickness, O night, again,
> Again this muffled flavor, this flavor of the depths,
> This far away flavor, this total flavor,
> This flavor where I feel the earth in a unique taste,
> This original flavor, source of all flavor,
> Sudden appearance of depths,
> Unique flavor.

3

THE SCENT OF THE
PRESENT MOMENT

THE INVISIBLE LANGUAGE
OF SMELL

Smell immerses us in an invisible language. Smells do not occupy any space at all, but they permeate our world. They hide themselves and reveal themselves. They have no shape or form and spread quickly. Smells tell us a lot about our surroundings and the human interactions going on around us, at different hours of the day and at different ages of life. They do all this in direct and indirect ways.

Smell is a fantastic foundation for interpreting life. Every moment has its smell. Each step. Each person. Smell imprints emotional meanings that help us differentiate one moment from another. Smell lacks concreteness, so we can only speak of it in metaphors, but, in reality, it is not abstract. When a person rubs a few drops of perfume on her skin, its aroma, even if produced in huge quantities by some company, nevertheless becomes specific to the person wearing it. The body makes all perfumes inimitable because it absorbs and expresses them in a unique way. This is how smell becomes a kind of topography, an intimate source of knowledge.

MY SMELL TELLS MY STORY

Through smell, we can perceive a kind of narration, an autobiographical story. My scent speaks of me. The smells imprinted in my memory are my emotional heritage, my history. Smell, and especially the first smell, that emerges with mere presence of someone, does not lie. Our scents, uniquely, don't share our edges or boundaries in space. Because they go beyond us, they allow us to spread, to open up, to dilute ourselves into the space around us in a way that would otherwise be impossible for us. And we need them. I remember hearing this question many years ago: "Is a perfume used to hide us or reveal us?"

SCENT, THE SOUL OF LIFE

Scent is an essential element in Greek literature on banquets. As you would expect, a scent is not just a scent. It can have a consoling character, as a verse from the Brazilian poet Alceu Valença suggests: "On the head that has suffered much / Spreads the scent."

Smell is a convivial habit associated with eating and drinking, as attested by Plutarch; it is a therapeutic way to reduce revulsion and mourning. (In one of the passages in *The Odyssey*, e.g., the handmaiden Eurynome urges Penelope to wear perfume to ease the pain of Ulysses's absence.) It can even symbolically illustrate the ideal life of a person, representing a moral challenge. Thus in Xenophon's *Symposium* (also known as the *Banquet*), when Lycon asks Socrates what a man's scent should be, the philosopher replies, "That of virtue and honor." Scent thus gains an existential and moral density: by scent, we arrive at the soul of life.

SMELL IS THE FIRST PRAYER

One might say that the Bible is read not only with the eyes, but also with the sense of smell. It is written both with words and with smells. Sometimes what verbal language doesn't say is conveyed by smell. This often happens in the biblical text. When no human speech expresses what one feels, scent intrudes as a manifestation of praise or as a cry.

In the Book of Exodus, God tells Moses to make an altar of acacia wood overlaid in pure gold. God says, "Aaron shall offer fragrant incense on it; every morning when he dresses the lamps he shall offer it, and when Aaron sets up the lamps in the evening, he shall offer it, a regular incense offering before the LORD throughout your generations" (Exod 30:7–8). The smell of the incense is a reminder of the covenant.

Throughout the Book of Exodus, whenever there is a reference to sacrifice, there is also reference to fragrance. Burning portions of meat or grain is not important in itself; what makes them meaningful, symbolically, is the smoke that rises from them. What goes up from them to the heavens? It is the smell, the warmth, its invisible expression that spreads like the desire to enter into relationship with the divine. The prayer that the people address to the Lord through the offering of their best animals and agricultural goods is, concretely, this fragrant cloud that fills the earth and rises to the heart of God. Smell is the first prayer. By combustion, the slain animals or the burnt grains end up becoming only an odor, an invisible prayer that rises to an invisible recipient. This is the offering.

FOR GOD, WE ARE A SMELL

In some prophetic texts we find an important element of the theme of smell. In the Book of the prophet Ezekiel, speaking of the people who will return from exile, God says, "As a pleasing odor I will accept you, when I bring you out from the peoples, and gather you out of the countries where you have been scattered; and I will manifest my holiness among you in the sight of the nations" (Ezek 20:41).

Here, clearly, the pleasant smell is not only that of the sacrificial meats or grains offered to the Lord; it is that of the people themselves. This is an important development in the prophetic literature. The smell of our herds or the dew on our fields is not enough for God. The smell that pleases God is that of the people, this evidence of their presence, this biography that is written intensely without a single word.

Later, in the New Testament, we find this expressed by Paul as well, but with a notable emphasis and a semantic force. In 2 Corinthians, Paul writes, "We are the aroma of Christ to God" (2 Cor 2:15). As in Ezekiel, Paul makes odor a metaphor for life. We are an aroma; the aroma is us, our *life*. It is the gift that God accepts. However, Paul says something that the prophet could not guess: if "we are the aroma of Christ to God," it means that it is Christ in us who allows the oblation, who guarantees the offering, who configures our life as a gift. What must enter us through the nostrils is this good news: we belong to Christ. More important than our smells, those that we carry in our memories, those of our present (which are always a mixture of intoxicating and repulsive) is Christ. It is through Christ, with Christ, and "in Christ" (a phrase that is central in Paul's theology) that we *are* this pleasant smell that rises to God: "Thanks be to God, who in Christ always leads us in triumphal procession, and through us spreads in every place the fragrance that comes from knowing him" (2 Cor 2:14).

READING WITH YOUR NOSE

The Song of Songs is a collection of smells, a mountain of aromas. It truly must be read with one's nose. No one can claim to have read and understood this absolutely central text in the Jewish and

Christian mystical tradition who have never inhaled the aroma of the freshly crushed juice of grapes or a pomegranate, mandrakes, figs or the skin of apples, beds of balms and lilies covered with dew, frankincense, myrrh, aloe, nard, saffron, straw, or cinnamon. Reading is more than understanding with one's eyes. Our olfactory memory is essential to feeling the intoxication of the adventure offered by this sacred text.

The two protagonists compare each other to a perfume, which shows the depth of knowledge they have of each other. One lover says to the other, "Your anointing oils are fragrant, / your name is perfume poured out; / therefore the maidens love you" (Song 1:3). Or: "My beloved is to me a bag of myrrh" (Song 1:13). The beloved responds by saying of his beloved, "What is that coming up from the wilderness, / like a column of smoke, / perfumed with myrrh and frankincense, / with all the fragrant powders of the merchant?" (Song 3:6).

To these two lovers, nothing seems to better express the quality of what they share than the suggestive catalogue of smells, which they constantly list: "How sweet is your love, my sister, my bride! / how much better is your love than wine, / and the fragrance of your oils than any spice!" (Song 4:10); "My beloved has gone down to his garden, / to the beds of spices" (Song 6:2). The odorous nature of the language of lovers speaks volumes about the radical opening of the senses released by the experience of love; indeed, it is also said of the Song of Songs that it is not only an olfactory dictionary; it is also a powerful visual grammar, a living laboratory of listening, a book of flavors, and an account of dazzling and difficult caresses.

It is also impressive to see how the love experience of these two people extends to the world around them. Sometimes we experience love as a radical indifference to what surrounds us, like a bubble of happiness; but that is not what this love is like. Their love makes them discover the extraordinary beauty of the world:

My beloved speaks and says to me:
"Arise, my love, my fair one,

and come away;
for now the winter is past,
   the rain is over and gone.
The flowers appear on the earth;
   the time of singing has come,
and the voice of the turtledove
   is heard in our land.
The fig tree puts forth its figs,
   and the vines are in blossom;
   they give forth fragrance.
Arise, my love, my fair one,
   and come away." (Song 2:10–13)

By reading—better: by *inhaling*—this book, we discover that we find ourselves before the absolute of love, which requires attention and expectation, as if we were living in a state of permanent alert. Love is more a longing than a possession, more of a plea than a gift, more a thirst than a dam, more a conversation of beggars than a dialogue of winners. It is by smell that we can learn something.

THE CONSOLATION OF SMELL

Fragrance is an expression of consolation where life is celebrated. It's another form of jubilation. It is praise without words, an intense melody that we hear without having to use hearing. Fragrance is music that is both silent and vibrant. The Bible offers us unforgettable examples. One of them comes to us in the form of a father's blessing for his son:

Then his father Isaac said to him, "Come near and kiss me, my son." So he came near and kissed him; and he smelled the smell of his garments, and blessed him, and said,

"Ah, the smell of my son
is like the smell of a field that the LORD has blessed."
(Gen 27:26–27)

Another example, just as striking, is the praise of fraternal communion that appears in the Psalms:

How very good and pleasant it is
when kindred live together in unity!
It is like the precious oil on the head,
running down upon the beard,
on the beard of Aaron,
running down over the collar of his robes. (Ps 133:1–2)

The image describes the graceful movement of perfumed oil, first poured over the head, which then runs over the beard, and then down to the bottom fringe of the garment.[1] In other words, from head to toes! The perfumed oil thus signals that family communion makes the whole body and one's whole life precious.

A final example among many we could have chosen is from the Book of Proverbs, which sings of the good smell of friendship: "Perfume and incense make the heart glad, / but the soul is torn by trouble" (Prov 27:9). Friendship perfumes our path in this common search for truth, beauty, and goodness.

FRAGRANCE AND HOSPITALITY

In consonance with Middle Eastern culture, biblical traditions are rich in references to fragrance. While they have the sacred meanings of which we have spoken, they are also found in more "secular" contexts. The use of fragrance constitutes one of the essential rites of hospitality because it communicates the joy of the encounter.

Fragrances are an important sign of the joy of living: "Perfume and incense make the heart glad," as we just read in Proverbs 27:9. They tell us about individuals: "Your robes are all fragrant with myrrh and aloes and cassia" (Ps 45:8). But they also reveal groups and peoples: "[They] drink wine from bowls, / and anoint themselves with the finest oils" (Amos 6:6).

The use of fragrances is an integral part of the rules of hospitality and banquets. When a guest arrives, the host welcomes them by perfuming their heads. Meanwhile, failing to present a bottle of perfume to one's host is considered offensive. In Genesis 18:4, Abraham proposes to perform the rituals of hospitality to his guest himself, beginning with the washing of the feet.

THE NECESSARY WASTE

It is interesting to note that, in the Gospels, *perfumes play a key role in the revelation of Jesus*. One might say that the Gospels' presentation of the Christian faith is olfactory.

In Mark's account, for example, we read, "While he was at Bethany in the house of Simon the leper, as he sat at the table, a woman came with an alabaster jar of very costly ointment of nard, and she broke open the jar and poured the ointment on his head" (Mark 14:3). What did this woman do? What did she claim to reveal? It turns out that she dared to say in a single gesture words that she had neither the time nor the space to express; this valuable nard that she poured over the head of this itinerant preacher was worth a thousand words. The languages of faith are necessarily plural; we forget that too often. This plurality is on display here. Smell is a kind of listening, but while listening is traditionally linked to verbal discourse, smell listens to silent language, faith that expresses itself without even needing to be named. There is no doubt that this woman staked everything on her gesture, that it took on a weight of meaning that did not go unnoticed by the guests who witnessed it.

One did not perfume a stranger by pure chance, did not pour such an expensive ointment for nothing. There is a meaning to which the unforgettable smell of this nard gives shape with its fragrance.

The rest of the story demonstrates vividly how risky and dramatic her action was:

> But some were there who said to one another in anger, "Why was the ointment wasted in this way? For this ointment could have been sold for more than three hundred denarii, and the money given to the poor." And they scolded her. But Jesus said, "Let her alone; why do you trouble her? She has performed a good service for me." (Mark 14:4–6)

"She has performed a good service for me." This comment from Jesus should make us aware of the goodness of what might otherwise seem to be only a waste. The truth is that we need not just bread, but also roses. On certain occasions, extravagance is not a deviant eccentricity; sometimes what is best is essential. It is common at times to reduce the spiritual life to what is necessary, to what we must do, to moral norms and obligations. It is common to avoid excess in favor of being frugal. All this is very good, no one can accuse us of anything, but it is our heart that accuses us: there is little love, little gratuitousness, little generosity, little surplus...and, though we try to hide it, the reality is this: where there is not an excess of love, there is no love. Loving means having no timetable, no schedule, no routine or measure. As St. Augustine reminded us, "The measure of love is to love without measure." There is no love without an experience of pure grace. We might say that an ointment is an extravagance because one can get along fine with water and a bit of soap, but then why did Jesus say, "She has performed a good service for me"?

The rest of the story also gives food for thought. Jesus pronounces this explanation:

For you always have the poor with you, and you can show kindness to them whenever you wish; but you will not always have me. She has done what she could; she has anointed my body beforehand for its burial. Truly I tell you, wherever the good news is proclaimed in the whole world, what she has done will be told in remembrance of her. (Mark 14:7–9)

Did the woman know that the ointment she poured was a messianic sign? Would she have been aware of the revolution represented by her choice to pour perfume on Jesus's head (an investiture that gives power to a chosen person), rather than on his feet? Did she intend, by her gesture, to anticipate the mystery of his death and resurrection? Maybe she didn't know or knew only partially. For her, it was a sign of love, care, and joy. For this reason, this woman, whose name we do not know, risks offering her expression of love before a group of strangers, spreading the scent of Jesus's identity.

A life lived in love will sometimes seem to us and to others a thousand times a waste. It then becomes like this precious perfume spread.

THE HOUSE WAS FILLED WITH THE FRAGRANCE OF THE PERFUME

We need to rediscover Mary of Bethany, that figure in the Gospel of John of a believer with an intensely personal and fragrant faith. Mary lived a relationship with Jesus based on friendship and multiple expressions of love, more a poetic expression than a formality. She is certainly a vibrant model of faith that invites us to reconsider our own sometimes strangely "odorless" faith. It is notable that Mary always appears in connection with olfactory symbolism. The evangelist begins by describing her as "the one who anointed the Lord with perfume and wiped his feet with her hair" (John 11:2). This is a first sign that her relationship with Jesus was not limited to a cerebral expression but takes shape through concrete and affective gestures.

The scene described in John 11 could not be more dramatic. Falling ill, Mary's brother Lazarus had died. She and her sister Martha had sent word to Jesus: "Lord, he whom you love is ill" (John 11:3). But Jesus was late, and when he arrived at Bethany, the worst had already happened. That's why, when Jesus asked that the tomb be opened, they replied, "Lord, already there is a stench because he has been dead four days" (John 11:39). On hearing that Jesus was entering the city, the sisters went out to meet him, apparently at separate moments. It is amazing to see in this story the difference between the two sisters.

The conversation with Martha is impressive from a theological point of view, and her trust in Jesus gives me chills. Let's listen to it:

> Martha said to Jesus, "Lord, if you had been here, my brother would not have died. But even now I know that God will give you whatever you ask of him." Jesus said to her, "Your brother will rise again." Martha said to him, "I know that he will rise again in the resurrection on the last day." Jesus said to her, "I am the resurrection and the life. Those who believe in me, even though they die, will live, and everyone who lives and believes in me will never die. Do you believe this?" She said to him, "Yes, Lord, I believe that you are the Messiah, the Son of God, the one coming into the world." (John 11:21–27)

The dialogue with Mary is equally profound but completely different. It is not a theoretical exchange about the nature of faith. It's an encounter, a revelation of her feelings, a consolation of physical presence, silence, and shared tears. Let's see what the text tells us:

Now Jesus had not yet come to the village, but was still at the place where Martha had met him. The Jews who were with her in the house, consoling her, saw Mary get up quickly and go out. They followed her because they thought that she was going to the tomb to weep there. When Mary came where Jesus was and saw him, she knelt at his feet and said to him, "Lord, if you had been here, my brother would not have died." When Jesus saw her weeping, and the Jews who came with her also weeping, he was greatly disturbed in spirit and deeply moved. He said, "Where have you laid him?" They said to him, "Lord, come and see." Jesus began to weep. (John 11:30–35)

We know the end of the story: Jesus raises Lazarus from the dead. But we usually fail to recognize the connection between this scene and the following one, which recounts the continuation of this friendship (in friendship, there is always a continuation). The friends are not only united in mourning; they also celebrate together trials overcome.

Lazarus, Martha, and Mary invite Jesus to a meal (John 12:2). We can imagine the joy and gratitude, all that is said and all that can never be adequately expressed. Where words and reason can't express themselves, the senses and symbols take over. Instead of having a servant wash her guest's feet, Mary takes care of it herself. The very brief description of the scene that the evangelist gives us shows that each member of the family expresses her or his faith in a unique and personal way. Let's see:

There they gave a dinner for him. Martha served, and Lazarus was one of those at the table with him. Mary took a pound of costly perfume made of pure nard, anointed Jesus' feet, and wiped them with her hair. The house was filled with the fragrance of the perfume. (John 12:2–3)

It is not a question of choosing one expression of love at the expense of others, but rather of drawing attention to different expressions that we might miss. Lazarus is sitting at his table, in the company of Jesus, perhaps in conversation with him. Martha is putting the finishing touches to the preparations for the meal. And Mary anoints the feet of Jesus. Mary's gestures, which we observe more closely here, transform the ordinary—the welcoming act of washing the dusty feet of a guest—into something extraordinary. An everyday gesture gains its nobility by the gratuitousness of the gift, by the excess of a love more precious than the most precious perfume. There is a necessity here that is no longer of the order of survival, but which expresses the fullness of life—blessed waste by which a grateful heart is known. Let us not be surprised, then, by this marvelous detail that the evangelist gives us: "The house was filled with the fragrance of the perfume" (John 12:3). Anyone who thinks this bit of information is an unimportant detail in the story's narrative doesn't understand the story at all.

THE SCENT OF FAITH

We know today that John's Gospel was not a first proclamation. Written later than the other three Gospels, it addresses a community that had already come a long way in its faith. This Gospel is an invitation to a deeper encounter, a more profound conversion. That's why it depicts not just the awakening of a relationship but what that relationship becomes.

For example, John mentions Nicodemus three times. In his first dialogue with Jesus, a nocturnal dialogue, Nicodemus stumbles forward, from surprise to surprise: "How can anyone be born after having grown old?...How can these things [to be born from above] be?" (John 3:4, 9). Although he is curious and interested in this conversation, he is also very afraid. He sought Jesus discreetly, so as not to be seen in his company. What he heard left him puzzled, but at the end of this encounter, we don't know what he concluded about it. If all we had was the account of this first meeting, we would not know whether Nicodemus had become a believer or not.

But we have two further passages. In the middle of the Gospel of John, Nicodemus takes the floor in front of everyone, to defend Jesus before the Sanhedrin. He asks, "Our law does not judge people without first giving them a hearing to find out what they are doing, does it?" (John 7:51). Then later, at the end of the Gospel, without any hesitation, Nicodemus appears again, with Joseph of Arimathea, to anoint the dead body of Jesus: "Nicodemus, who had at first come to Jesus by night, also came, bringing a mixture of myrrh and aloes, weighing about a hundred pounds" (John 19:39). Certainly, the tradition of the Jews was to anoint the body of someone who had died with perfume—but not with such a huge amount. This attention to the body of Jesus, this way of taking care of it, this excess, is Nicodemus's prayer. It's the scent of his own faith.

THE NOSE IN THE BIBLE

In the Bible, the nose is the seat of irascibility, fury, and indignation. In this context, we find metaphors relating to fire, which express well the consuming passion that is at stake: anger is a fire that devours, that burns. For example, in Judges we read, "The anger of the LORD was kindled against Israel" (3:8)—and here a common Portuguese translation renders this as "The Lord's nose caught fire against Israel." This way of putting it relates to an amusing expression that we find in both Portuguese and in French. To refer to progressively getting angry and losing one's temper, one speaks of *avoir la moutarde qui monte au nez*, that is, "having the mustard go up one's nose." It refers, of course, to the burning irritation and flushed skin that one might experience in such a case.

AROMA AND SACRED PLACES

The Bible lists seven different kinds of incense; this is indicative of the great attention it pays to smell. In the Book of Exodus, it is God himself who teaches Moses how to make holy oil from selected perfumes:

> The LORD spoke to Moses: Take the finest spices: of liquid myrrh five hundred shekels, and of sweet-smelling cinnamon half as much, that is, two hundred fifty, and two hundred fifty of aromatic cane, and five hundred of cassia—measured by the sanctuary shekel—and a hin of olive oil; and you shall make of these a sacred anointing oil blended as by the perfumer; it shall be a holy anointing oil. (Exod 30:22–25)

Historically, aromatic substances have been used in divine worship and have been the starting point for analogies of great theological intensity, for example, when prayer is compared to the smoke of incense rising to the sky: "Let my prayer be counted as incense before you" (Ps 141:2). In the New Testament, the Letter to the Ephesians goes a step further in the comparison with the perfume, when Paul writes, "Live in love, as Christ loved us and gave himself up for us, a fragrant offering and sacrifice to God" (Eph 5:2).

We might recall our own experience of visiting sacred places and the olfactory perception of the mystery that they often include. Montaigne's sixteenth-century *Essays* offer an interesting testimony on this subject:

> Physicians might, I believe, extract greater utility from odors than they do, for I have often observed that they cause an alteration in me and work upon my spirits according to their several virtues; which makes me approve of what is said, that the use of incense and perfumes in churches, so

ancient and so universally received in all nations and religions, was intended to cheer us, and to rouse and purify the senses, the better to fit us for contemplation.[2]

THE SUPPRESSION OF SMELL

In an essay on the anthropology of smell, David Le Breton writes that Western societies have stopped valuing odors. He gives two examples. Five hundred years ago, the German language included at least 158 words to describe various smells and aromas. Only thirty-two survive today, often in very localized, dialect forms. At the same time, in the Arab-Muslim world, which keeps the wisdom of smells alive, there are about 250 such terms. Smells characterize all areas of Middle Eastern life, from the most trivial to the most important. Of course, they usually overflow from inside houses out into the streets.

The American anthropologist Edward T. Hall, who studied nonverbal communication, observed the phenomenon of *the suppression of smell* in American society. He wrote, "In the use of the olfactory apparatus, Americans are culturally underdeveloped. The extensive use of deodorants and the suppression of odor in public places results in a land of olfactory blandness and sameness that would be difficult to duplicate anywhere else in the world. This blandness makes for undifferentiated spaces and deprives us of richness and variety in life."[3]

SOCIAL CONTROL OF ODORS

Freud associated the decline of regard for odors in Western culture with the progress of our civilization and societies. He says smell has lost importance in favor of sight. Smell is too close to our primitive states, excessively exposing us to individuality, reminding us too much of our bodiliness.

Today we have a great deal of insecurity about the aromas that emanate from our bodies. Advertising makes this shame more acute to get us to buy deodorants and perfumes. We strive to hide our natural odors, and we go to great lengths to redesign the olfactory landscapes in which we live and work. An entire industry has developed to control the smells of our environment, creating specific aromas for the various parts of the house or the car, using sprays and little machines to spray them automatically and regularly, sticks of incense, liquids that imitate the smell of pine or lavender, even as our lifestyles take us further and further from nature. Our sense of smell, trapped in the demands of commerce, becomes more controlled, but also more artificial.

Sometimes what we need in our homes isn't an odor neutralizer, but the more frequent opening of windows.

SMELL AND MEMORY

"Smell is a strange kind of seeing. It evokes sentimental landscapes through a rapid sketching done by the subconscious. I've felt this very often," confessed Fernando Pessoa in his masterwork *The Book of Disquiet*.[4] One odor is, in fact, sufficient to pull us far into the details of an intimate story. It mobilizes our awareness and our memory in a way that can last an extremely long time. Sometimes, touched by the hint of an odor, our eyes might widen with a smile of delight or fill with tears of sadness. Odors pull us back in time and inside ourselves. They are an internal instrument of reminiscence. Our memory is a palette of smells.

The novelist Marcel Proust, whose work teaches us so much about the senses, wrote, "When nothing subsists from an old past, after the death of people, after the destruction of things, alone, frailer but more enduring, more immaterial, more persistent, smell and taste remain for a long time, like souls, remembering, waiting, hoping, upon the ruins of all the rest, hearing without giving way, on their almost impalpable droplet, the immense edifice of memory."[5]

THE AROMA OF COFFEE

Describing an odor is impossible to do with precision; we mostly have only metaphors and comparisons. This passage from Wittgenstein's *Philosophical Investigations* well expresses this difficulty: "Describe the aroma of coffee—why can't it be done? Do we lack the words? And *for what* are words lacking?—But how do we get the idea that such a description must after all be possible? Have you ever felt the lack of such a description? Have you tried to describe the aroma of coffee and not succeeded?"[6]

SMELL PROTECTS US

How many times has a smell protected us? It is by smell that we realize that we have forgotten something in the oven or that some strange element has entered the area where we are. The smell of acid or the stench coming from spoiled food warns us. Before a baby can talk, odors help the parents take care of it. In many societies, aromas and scents from the plant world or of certain substances are linked to common therapeutic practices. Through vapors or sprays, aromas purify spaces, fight diseases, and restore the body's defenses.

A DYSTOPIA

In his *Dictionnaire du XXIe siècle* (Dictionary of the Twenty-First Century), the French writer Jacques Attali comments that we urban nomads fail to even notice the decline in our olfactory capacities, simply because we so rarely use them. But the Big Brother of the future will have to invest its control of them, if it understands the extraordinary world of the hidden possibilities of smell. So Attali imagines a kind of dystopia: the day when we can digitize the sense of smell, the door will be open to all kinds of manipulations. Odors will become an instrument of propaganda and submission. When androids can emit odors, the virtual will be completely confused with the real. This day, Attali insists, will certainly come.

SMALL EPIPHANIES

The ability to be silent and pay attention may be the most essential element in the daily progress of a journey of faith. Light a candle, take a different route, enjoy a quiet walk without worrying about how long it lasts or the next thing that needs to happen, stop when you normally would not and breathe in the scent of the present moment. These are small epiphanies of grace that can transform one's life. Spiritualities need open windows because they quickly tend to develop in a cocoon, far from the unfettered breath of the Holy Spirit. They need gusts of wonder that tell us the following: "Give thanks for the luminous dance of the world around you." "Make a promise to address unfinished business." "It's when you give your life away that it truly becomes yours." "Don't hide from the light."

This concern for fragrance can seem superficial and frivolous. But recall what G. K. Chesterton wrote in his book *Orthodoxy*: "Seriousness is not a virtue." He continued, "It would be a heresy, but a much more sensible heresy, to say that seriousness is a vice. It is really a natural trend or lapse into taking one's self gravely, because it is the easiest thing to do. It is much easier to write a good *Times* leading article than a good joke in [the popular humor magazine] *Punch*. For solemnity flows out of men naturally; but laughter is a leap."[7] Humor can open up a space for wisdom.

PATIENCE: SMELL THE PRESENT MOMENT

Suddenly, we find ourselves having trouble dealing with the unfinished and the "raw" aspects of life, with growth and development and its unevenness, with the advances and setbacks necessary for learning. We approach all of life with the same impatience as when we wait in heavy traffic or stand in line at some administrative office. We become prisoners of a tightly closed universe, unable to notice the opening that the scent of life insists on offering us.

Suddenly, we find ourselves knowing how to measure time only by a clock and to think that we have no time to lose. The clock's time is regulated mechanically or digitally. It is neutral and painless, meaningless and uniform; it runs, unalterable, always forward, indifferent to the interference of the present or to what remains behind. The time of the clock is simple and continuous, insisting that it must continue at any cost. It is time without attachment, without feelings that delay, without roots that ripen. Clock time is not exactly human time. Despite everything, we have made its power a sort of absolute rule of civilization.

I would say that the exercise of patience begins with an acceptance of a life full of hope. It confronts us with vulnerability—ours and that of others. Probably we still feel distant from our goals; we do not like everything that we find in ourselves or around us; we perceive that a work of transformation must continue or even intensify. Patience should not be confused with indecision, passivity, or a lack of courage. On the contrary: patience is the audacity not to be instrumentalized by haste or blocked by fear, but to actively invest our time in the management of complex and unexpected expressions of life, and this with wisdom, serenity, and a constructive attitude. I love the way St. Thomas Aquinas explains patience. Patience, he says, is the ability not to despair.[8]

After planting a seed, the farmer does not desperately dig at the earth to check it. She must be detached from it, knowing that there is a necessary time of waiting so that the seed, in nature's rhythm, can grow. The fisherman does not abandon the sea forever only because that day he was unable to catch any fish. He knows there is only one thing to do: come back the next day.

Patience means paying attention to the opportunity and the singularity of each moment, with the full awareness that our lives are built from a variety of materials: various origins, memories of all kinds, different companions, bits of this or that. We can only realize our personal unity and our communion with others in the unexpected encounter of diversity, through a long life of listening, availability, effective recognition, negotiation, and, ultimately, encounter. Most of the time, we live amidst unfinished business. Patience, if we want it, is the art of welcoming this unfinished business and making it the starting point of ceaseless work to give it new meaning. It is largely a work of reconciliation.

The nineteenth-century Italian writer Giacomo Leopardi reminded us, not without a touch of humor, "Patience is the most heroic of the virtues precisely because it has not the least appearance of heroism."[9] I also see some humor in the fact that the Greek word for patience, *makrothymia*, basically describes a way of breathing. In Greek, patience is a long, relaxed, and open breath, unlike our hurried and even suffocating breathing. Maybe all we must do is stop, inhale, and smell the fragrance of the present moment.

4

LISTEN TO THE MELODY OF THE PRESENT MOMENT

THE EAR OF YOUR HEART

Listening is perhaps the sense that best demonstrates that we have accepted the complexity of life. Too many of us listen too infrequently. Among the skills we develop in life, the art of listening is often missing. The Rule of St. Benedict contains an essential expression for those who want to understand how to truly listen: "Listen carefully...with the ear of your heart."[1]

Real listening, in other words, is done not only with our physical, exterior ears, but with our heart. Listening is not just collecting the noise or words in the air around us. Above all, it is an attitude. It bows to the other; it is ready to welcome what is said and what is not said, the enthusiasm of history or its opposite, its pain.

WHEN DUST HEARS BREATH

What was the very first noise we heard? We now know that by the third month of pregnancy, a baby in the womb is already able to hear sounds. He or she hears the human voice for the first time and perceives outside noises.

In this light, we might say that the first thing that humans heard was the breath of God: "Then the LORD God formed man from the dust of the ground, and breathed into his nostrils the breath of life; and the man became a living being" (Gen 2:7). The dust received the breath of eternity. This is where our great adventure started. Clearly what is dust in us will one day become dust again, but it will be more. As the verse from Françisco de Quevedo's poem says, "Dust [my body] shall be. That dust will be in love."[2]

LISTENING IS A FORM OF HOSPITALITY

Spiritual knowledge is not the result of our accumulation of historical and theological information. The wisdom that is most decisive in one's life comes from listening. In a way, this is what Jesus reminds Peter immediately after his great confession of Caesarea: "Blessed are you, Simon son of Jonah! For flesh and blood has not revealed this to you, but my Father in heaven" (Matt 16:17). There is an existential learning that is only received through hearing.

In this sense also, Jesus's encounter with his friends in Bethany—Lazarus, Martha, and Mary—is exemplary. Mary sat at the feet of Jesus, illustrating the attitude of listening that characterizes the disciple. Her sister Martha was busy in the kitchen, far from her host. Jesus was clear: "Mary has chosen the better part, which will not be taken away from her" (Luke 10:42). At some point in our lives, we understand that basic knowledge comes from listening, which is the most needed form of hospitality.

LISTENING TO THE FOREST GROW

Listening strengthens our ability to hear. We know that a falling tree makes more noise than a growing forest. A truck running near empty or half full makes more noise than if it has a full tank of gas. A vacuum can be noisy. Half tanks, like half-truths, are more likely to cause friction.

One of the early desert fathers said that the listening capacity of one of his disciples was so great that he could hear a falling needle from a distance of seven meters. Very often, however, we ourselves would be unable to hear it from seven centimeters. For this reason, listening requires practice and training. Our ears have become numb. We can hear, but we don't listen. "Mortal, you are living in the midst of a rebellious house, who have eyes to see but do not see, who have ears to hear but do not hear," says the prophet Ezekiel (Ezek 12:2). So much is waiting to be heard, and we simply do not listen!

Listening requires a rootedness, a *habitus*, a permanence. Certainly, one can be full of ambiguities, and we need a "school of listening." Recall the story of young Samuel (1 Sam 3), who hears his name called but does not realize it is God calling him; he thinks he hears the voice of Elijah, his master. This is a story of learning to listen. It speaks of an inner alertness that we can learn gradually, a disposition of the heart that allows us to hear what is inaudible. Let's be clear: everything we listen to, absolutely everything, should only be a preparation for listening to what remains silent. It is only through the habit of silence—long, daily times of silence and exposure to God in prayer—that listening can mature.

WANDERING JOY

There was a great wind, so strong that it was splitting mountains and breaking rocks in pieces before the LORD, but the LORD was not in the wind; and after the wind an earthquake, but the LORD was not in the earthquake; and after the earthquake a fire, but the LORD was not in the fire; and after the fire a sound of sheer silence. When Elijah heard it, he wrapped his face in his mantle and went out and stood at the entrance of the cave. (1 Kgs 19:11–13)

We must learn to exchange power for the lightness of a breath, like Elijah. We must exchange all the noise for the murmur of silence, before which Elijah covers his face; to be like the herds in the fields that follow the melody of the shepherd's flute, without which they would not know their wandering joy.

LISTENING IS THE FLAVOR OF PRESENCE

When we compare the two Gospel accounts of the baptism of Jesus and his transfiguration, what we find is fundamentally the same statement from heaven. At his baptism, we hear a voice that says, "You are my Son, the Beloved; with you I am well pleased" (Mark 1:11; Luke 3:22), or, as Matthew reports it, "This is my Son, the Beloved, with whom I am well pleased" (Matt 3:17). Then, in the story of the transfiguration, we find the repetition of these same words, but with a single notable change: the introduction of the imperative tense, the command to "Listen!" In Mark's version, we have the following: "This is my Son, the Beloved; listen to him!" (Mark 9:7). In Matthew's: "This is my Son, the Beloved; with him I am well pleased; listen to him!" (Matt 17:5). And in Luke's: "This is my Son, my Chosen; listen to him!" (Luke 9:35). The appearance of the verb *listen* at this precise moment not only illuminates the deep meaning of the episode of the transfiguration; it also opens perspectives on the very semantics of the verb itself.

The transfiguration scene occurs at a particularly sensitive stage in Jesus's journey with his disciples. They accompanied him, but they remained behind at important moments, when they found themselves disappointed, apprehensive, fearful of the consequences of what they were seeing, vacillating, and doubtful. Immediately after Peter's important confession—"You are the Messiah, the Son of the living God" (Matt 16:16)—the apostle rejects the fate that Jesus says awaits him: "God forbid it, Lord! This must never happen to you" (Matt 16:22). This shows how easily fear can overpower a disciple's trust in Jesus. Of course, what Peter basically meant was, "Lord, I don't want this to happen to me, to us." He was afraid for Jesus, but especially for himself.

So what is listening? It is the experience that will tear the scandal of the cross from the hearts of the disciples. There is no faith that does not arise from listening, from deep listening, from listening to the end. Listening is the place where Jesus can act, healing us from our fear. It is a listening without which we cannot live; this is real listening.

Oddly enough, in the transfiguration passages, when the Father's voice says "Listen," Jesus is not talking. The meaning of this "Listen" is this: "Welcome him. Receive the person of Jesus. Open yourselves to his mystery." It is not enough to have knowledge, to know, or simply to have in mind the truths we believe in. What is necessary is the listening that makes Jesus present with his plan and his destiny. By such listening, the Word that awakens and directs envelops us. We are led, we are healed. Listening places us not only in front of him, but also with him and in him. Without this listening, the Word remains in the distant past, his Passover is an event that does not enter the present moment. Listening gives us a taste for presence.

HEARING THE GOSPEL

In the biblical tradition, listening is very much related to faith. Listening is where faith takes root. Without listening, faith risks becoming an irrelevant set of words and gestures, or a code of good intentions. Jesus is clear about this:

> I will show you what someone is like who comes to me, hears my words, and acts on them. That one is like a man building a house, who dug deeply and laid the foundation on rock; when a flood arose, the river burst against that house but could not shake it, because it had been well built. But the one who hears and does not act is like a man who built a house on the ground without a foundation. When the river burst against it, immediately it fell, and great was the ruin of that house. (Luke 6:47–49)

Hearing, then, becomes living. It translates what is heard into concrete actions. It shapes our life. It is listening to shape this clay that we are, listening to build, to dream, to exist. We shouldn't miss the fact that Jesus does not tell us that whoever listens to his words will be spared from troubles, crises, dark nights, devastations, or suffering. The one who builds on sand is in the same situation as one who builds on rock: the storm hits both and the ground shakes under the feet of both. The only difference is how they stand the test.

I remember the words of a prior of a young monastic community with whom I was in contact. At one point in the conversation, I asked him, "Right now the community is young and full of strength. It bears the fragrance of springtime. But are you afraid of winter?"

I won't forget his reply: "We know the crisis is coming. We are living in a moment of extraordinary vitality right now, but the test will come. The only thing we ask the Lord is that when the crisis comes, we will be found listening to the gospel."

OBEDIENCE IS LISTENING

Whatever programs, projects, or dreams we have, everything must happen through the course of time. Everything must be purified like gold, and everything will be transformed. We must have a firm axis. This axis is listening to the gospel.

The choice to follow Jesus does not save us from suffering; it gives us the capacity to accept suffering with trust. We can do this only when we are rooted in listening. This is what evangelical obedience means. In Latin, the word meaning "obey," *ab-audire*, literally means "to open one's ears, to hear well, to listen carefully."

In the wonderful hymn of the Letter to the Philippians, St. Paul writes of Jesus, "He humbled himself / and became obedient to the point of death— / even death on a cross" (Phil 2:8). This obedience that becomes a gift of oneself, a radical offering of one's own life, arises from a loving relationship that is listening. We can know the heart of a person by what he says, but also by what he listens to. Jesus said to his disciples, "I do not call you servants any longer, because the servant does not know what the master is doing; but I have called you friends, because I have made known to you everything that I have heard from my Father" (John 15:15).

"LET ANYONE WITH EARS LISTEN!"

There is a phrase that Jesus repeats often, at the end of a parable or a teaching, to the point that it is a typical expression of his speech: "Let anyone with ears listen!" (Matt 11:15; Mark 4:9; etc.). It is interesting to note that we find a similar phrase repeated in the Book of Revelation, at the conclusion of each of the seven letters to the seven churches of Asia: "Let anyone who has an ear listen to what the Spirit is saying to the churches" (Rev 2:7, 11, 17, 29; 3:6, 13, 22). Listening to the Spirit is a great challenge!

In the Gospel of John, Jesus, when he announces to his disciples that he is going to the Father, also tells them that he will send the Spirit, the consoling Spirit, who will lead them to the truth (see John 14:16–17, 26). What the disciples did not yet understand about Jesus, they will understand as they open themselves to the Spirit.

Peter's case is a paradigm. The Spirit brings about a revolution in this fearful and reluctant man, clinging to the firm ground of his certainties. When Peter goes to Cornelius and sees that the Holy Spirit was poured out on the pagans before they were even baptized, his point of view completely changes: "Can anyone withhold the water for baptizing these people who have received the Holy Spirit just as we have?" (Acts 10:47). The Acts of the Apostles demonstrates that the true protagonist in the history of the church is the Holy Spirit.

It is the Spirit who builds the church and guides the lives of Christians. The Spirit tells us the truth about Jesus, testifying in our hearts that Jesus is Lord. Listening to Jesus is not a disembodied exercise. On the contrary, it is a listening that transforms the church, purifies it, shakes it up, teaches it to live in hope. Opening up to listen to the Spirit is not about detecting rare and subtle signals; it means looking at how, in concrete terms, the gospel challenges my life. Reading the letters to the churches in the Book of Revelation is uncomfortable because they touch what is painful and hidden in us. Consider, for example, what is said to the church in Ephesus:

> I know your works, your toil and your patient endurance. I know that you cannot tolerate evildoers; you have tested those who claim to be apostles but are not,

and have found them to be false. I also know that you are enduring patiently and bearing up for the sake of my name, and that you have not grown weary. But I have this against you, that you have abandoned the love you had at first. (Rev 2:2–4)

Or to the church in Sardis: "Remember then what you received and heard; obey it, and repent" (Rev 3:3). Listening to the Spirit is an opening to the transformation of our life by the gospel, in docility to the paschal impulse: "Let anyone who has an ear listen to what the Spirit is saying to the churches." Listening is a sense of reality that is sometimes lacking in our faith. Without it, we'll fail to live a committed and engaged daily life.

GO DEAF AND YOU WILL HEAR

Here is a paradox that we must face: true listening requires that we become deaf. This is what the fourth-century master of the interior life Evagrius Ponticus teaches us: "Strive to keep your mind deaf during prayer time; and then you will be able to pray."[3]

What does he mean by this? For Evagrius, keeping one's mind "deaf" means proceeding with abandonment, letting go. Our listening is interrupted so often by false urgencies, fictions that invade us and prevent us from living in the present moment. When we are distracted like this in our listening and turn our attention to these things, we ignore what is important. This is why Evagrius recommends, "Go deaf." The truth is, if we are not able to, we will not dive into the silent ocean of listening.

Among the stories of the desert fathers, we find one about the disciple who, on entering the holy place for prayer, realizes that a bee has entered with him. As he tries to pray, the bee buzzes around his head. The disciple then gets up and goes to his master to explain that he can't pray because he is distracted and even frightened by this bee. The master replies, "Go and pray, don't stop praying, because even if the bee stings you, you will be alright." The most important thing is that this movement of listening, this fragile but powerful thread that ties us to life even if we do not realize it, does not break. This is what prompted another figure of desert spirituality to say, "If a man does not say in his heart, 'God and I are alone in the world,' he will never find peace."

A FORGOTTEN LISTENING

We easily fall into a legalistic and fragmentary conception of the experience of God; the remedy for this is love. The First Letter of John leaves no doubt: "No one has ever seen God; if we love one another, God lives in us, and his love is perfected in us" (1 John 4:12).

Love is paradoxical; it leads us to organize our life based on the paradox. The one who loves takes the risk of this contradiction, which consists in making an essential path one that most people avoid; it means following the teacher of the Beatitudes—blessed are the poor in spirit, the meek, the persecuted, and so on—who ended up on the cross. To do this, we must learn not to be afraid of this uncomfortable truth spoken by the psychoanalyst Jacques Lacan: "Love is giving what you do not have."

We are used to believing in the power of possession and abundance. Let us discover the hidden possibilities in simply being, in the radical poverty of life, in the rarity of visions, in the murmur covered by loud rhetoric, in the hidden listening that we also owe to the visible world. In 2 Corinthians, St. Paul wrote something that seems absurd: Christ, who was rich, made himself poor to enrich us (see 2 Cor 8:9). So what is this trust that Jesus places in the power of poverty?

LISTENING IS AN ACT OF RESISTANCE

The spiritual ear holds a memory. It holds the Word within itself. This is what the Gospel of Luke tells us about Mary. What she understood (and what she did not understand) of what she heard from Jesus, she kept in her heart, constantly meditating on it (see Luke 2:19). The Christian tradition invites us to discover listening as a *rumination*, the patient and incessant work of assimilating the mystery.

In an "avalanche" culture like ours, real listening can only take place by taking a critical step back from the frenzy of words and messages that seek to imprison us every minute. The lifestyles imposed on us are dizzying. To compensate for our exhausted lives, we seek distractions. The very word *distract* is revealing—it comes from the Latin *distrahere*, which means "to draw in various directions." To be distracted means to not be in one's own place, not to be anywhere, to be, rather, in a no-man's-land that is both our home and our exile.

This is why the art of listening is *an exercise in resistance*. Listening establishes a break with illusory reality, the idle succession of contacts, the torrent spilled by daily news transformed into a soap opera (whether it be political, economic, or cultural). Listening is sometimes a break, a symbolic disengagement, a refusal, stepping out of the whirlwind. One thing is certain: without it, our life is quickly invaded, colonized; it no longer belongs to us. Ironically, our communication society has a listening deficit.

A magnificent text by the late nineteenth- and early twentieth-century Bengali writer and artist Rabindranath Tagore describes well the way we are incapacitated when we delay our exodus, when we avoid breaking free from what ensnares us:

> The tame bird was in a cage, the free bird was in the
> forest.
> They met when the time came, it was a decree of fate.

The free bird cries, "O my love, let us fly to the wood."
The cage bird whispers, "Come hither, let us both live
in the cage."
Says the free bird, "Among bars, where is there room to
spread one's wings?"
"Alas," cries the cage bird, "I should not know where to
sit perched in the sky."

The free bird cries, "My darling, sing the songs of the
woodlands."
The cage bird sings, "Sit by my side, I'll teach you the
speech of the learned."
The forest bird cries, "No, ah no! songs can never be
taught."
The cage bird says, "Alas for me, I know not the songs
of the woodlands."

There love is intense with longing, but they never can
fly wing to wing.
Through the bars of the cage they look, and vain is their
wish to know each other.
They flutter their wings in yearning, and sing, "Come
closer, my love!"
The free bird cries, "It cannot be, I fear the closed doors
of the cage."
The cage bird whispers, "Alas, my wings are powerless
and dead."[4]

LOVE THE ONE WHO REALLY LISTENS TO YOU

Listening is related to alertness, promptness. Those who listen
put in place an inner vigilance that allows them to act with diligence

that never ceases to surprise. It is like athletes on the starting line, waiting for the signal. The quality of listening determines the quality of the response.

Here is another story from the desert fathers. A master had twelve disciples. His favorite was the one who takes care of calligraphy. Naturally, the others, who did not understand the master's predilection for him, were jealous. The master then decided to test them. One day when they were all busy working, each in his cell, the master called out, "My disciples, come here!" The first to respond was the calligrapher, and only afterward, gradually, the others arrived. Then the master led them to the calligrapher's cell, pointed to the word on the paper he'd been working on, and said to them, "Look. He was there writing the letter omega, and he interrupted it to respond to his master's call." Then the disciples replied, "Now we understand. You love the one who truly listens to you."

HEAR THE SILENCE

Sometimes what brings us closer to authenticity is to continue; sometimes it's to stop. We will only know which through patient practice and always listening. However, this listening is not done without courage or without death to ourselves. Nor can we wait for ideal conditions. I agree with what musician John Cage wrote: nowhere in time or in space does there truly exist what we call silence. Around us, everything is sound, if indeed we seek silence. Franz Kafka wrote a similar thing in reference to the self-revelatory process of writing: "This is why one can never be alone enough when one writes, why there can never be enough silence around one when one writes, why even night is not night enough."[5] What we call silence becomes real and effective only through a process of interior self-emptying. There is no other way.

The desert fathers teach us this with wisdom tinged with humor, as evidenced by this story of a monk named Arsenius:

One day Abba Arsenius came to a place where there were reeds blowing in the wind. The old man said to the brothers, "What is this movement?" They said, "Some reeds." Then the old man said to them, "When one who is living in silent prayer hears the song of a little sparrow, his heart no longer experiences the same peace. How much worse is it when you hear the movement of those reeds."[6]

Silence is not only external. One must have "silence of the heart," but this silence requires of us, every day, a firm decision and perseverance. The desert father Anthony said, "One who sits in solitude and is quiet has escaped from three wars: hearing, speaking, seeing. Yet against one thing shall he continually battle: that is, his own heart."[7]

LEARNING TO LISTEN TO WHAT WE SEEK

I will be the first to admit that few things give me as much pleasure, when I travel, as visiting familiar places where I will recognize people and be recognized, engaging in conversation with some folks who, over time, have almost become friends. In a city, a known face, even that of a stranger, is like an anchor. We feel a familiarity that brings peace. The French novelist Marguerite Yourcenar asked wisely, "How does one live without strangers around?" The reverse is also true.

One such familiar face that I've always found in Rome is that of a particular beggar. I have encountered him again and again for so many years! It is always impossible not to notice him—at the entrance to the university, the library, the cinema, Campo de' Fiori, St. Peter's Square, everywhere. Day and night. He must be sixty years old as I write this, a discreet and even delicate presence. I came to notice that he addresses passers-by with two questions: "Do you speak Italian?" he begins. Whatever the answer, he goes to the next step. He carefully takes a coin between two fingers, holds it up, and asks, "Do you have a hundred lira?" That's how I got to know him. When Italy later switched to the euro, he asked for ten cents.

The first time I encountered him with this request, I thought he was looking to supplement the price of a metro ticket or a slice of pizza. After meeting him dozens of times, I wasn't sure what to think, but I witnessed a scene that may partly solve this conundrum. On a street near the Pantheon, another beggar was sitting—lying down, in fact. His clothes were in tatters, growths deformed his arm, his face expressed pain and exclusion. From afar, I watched this beggar I knew approach him. To my amazement, I saw him repeat the questions he says to everyone, insistently showing him a coin. Whether it was to get the man to leave him alone or out of compassion, I saw the other beggar take a coin from his saucer to give it to him. It was there that the scene became unforgettable. The beggar I knew knelt there, took the other man's hands in his own, and kissed them several times, overcome with emotion. I think I finally understood. It was not the coins he wanted. It was a rare but vital good: the gift.

THE MUSIC IS EASY TO HEAR

There is a resemblance, a kind of interior relationship, between musical listening and spiritual listening. Martin Luther understood this clearly through St. Paul's comment in the Letter to the Romans, "Faith comes from what is heard" (10:17), and he made it the foundation of his theology of music.

Two aspects underline this affinity. The first is the *kind* of knowledge that these two types of listening communicate. The second is the paradoxical relationship they establish between the finite and the infinite.

Music has value in itself; strictly speaking, it does not try to convey a "message" or know how to transmit. It tells us nothing about the world but is a way of inhabiting this world. Its essence is rhythmic and not conceptual. It can be listened to simply, and that is its mode of communication. It is because it gives itself up to be heard that it finally makes us present to ourselves. Now, it is this same effect that produces spiritual listening—an awakening of consciousness, an attention to the present moment, an ability to register in the here and now.

On the other hand, music puts before us a paradox: the musician is a kind of ascetic. Her art requires maximum concentration, demanding from her scrupulous fidelity to a score and hours and hours of perseverance in reclusive solitude. All this rigor is only there to transform into lightness, pure play, letting go. Music tells us that the indivisible spreads into the divisible, that the infinite crosses the finite, that the indiscernible is the supreme expression of all that is audible. Isn't that what the listening of faith aspires to? In a double proposition, St. Paul tells us, "Faith comes from what is heard" (Rom 10:17) and "What no eye has seen, nor ear heard, / nor the human heart conceived, / what God has prepared for those who love him" (1 Cor 2:9). Faith opens to the indescribable.

Pope Benedict XVI, a great lover of music, offered a strong evocation of the effect of listening to a song by one of his favorite composers:

> When we listen to a piece of sacred music that plucks at our heartstrings, our mind, as it were, expands and turns naturally to God. I remember a concert of music by Johann Sebastian Bach in Munich, conducted by Leonard Bernstein. At the end of the last passage, one of the Cantatas, I felt, not by reasoning but in the depths of my heart, that what I had heard had communicated truth to me, the truth of the supreme composer, and impelled me to thank God. The Lutheran bishop of Munich was next to me and I said to him spontaneously: "In hearing this one understands: it is true; such strong faith is true, as

119

well as the beauty that irresistibly expresses the presence of God's truth."[8]

THE VOICE OF REALITY

Our personal experience has a certain value, but we show it off as if it were everything; we absolutize it. We find ourselves slandering and judging based solely on our own experience, on what has happened to us, both good and bad. It is necessary for us to understand the limits of our own experience, however, and to keep this in perspective, because though it is true, it is also biased. We must return to this leitmotif of the Letter to the Galatians: "For freedom Christ has set us free" (5:1). He freed us from our memory, our past, our knowledge, in relation to our experience. If we can say, "I've seen a lot, I know," what do we really know? Have we touched the bottom of things already? It reminds me of God's words to Job:

> Where were you when I laid the foundation of the
> earth?...
> Have you commanded the morning since your days
> began,
> and caused the dawn to know its place?...
> Where is the way to the dwelling of light,
> and where is the place of darkness? (Job 38:4, 12, 19)

Listen to these questions and welcome the voice of reality.

WHAT REMAINS TO BE SAID

A compass points north. It is oriented to the planet's North Pole. If a hiker pulls a compass from her backpack and finds that it's broken, however, it wouldn't occur to her to question the existence of north.

I offer this as a metaphor. There was a time when certain primary sources of meaning (religious, political, and ethical) provided an essential orientation for those who sought it. These sources of meaning had the clarity of a compass needle, and the answers they offered seemed simple, natural, and indisputable.

Nevertheless, powerful cultural changes and ruptures have brought us into a period that we can describe, continuing our metaphor, as follows: In our travels, we've stopped using the compass and turned to radar. That is, we no longer find our way in relation to a specific direction. It is true that radar is used to locate a particular object, but this quest is now more open, plural, moveable, and without predetermined orientations. The compass clearly indicated only one direction—north; radar brings both power and complexity to one's quest. The signals have diversified and the paths have multiplied. The paths of spiritual searching are no longer singular.

Today we face yet another change, because not only are we engaged in locating signals, but we are guaranteed the possibility of receiving them. If in the past we used radar to locate a signal, today we receive data without having to seek it out. Data (an email, for example) is received automatically because we have kept a reception channel open. Our challenge is not to find a meaningful message but to understand it.

The times are changing. Let's not forget that times of change bring growth. Winter is a season of preparation for new spring flowers. What can we learn? This is the necessary question. What does this cultural avalanche reveal to us? In fact, the most acute crisis is not that of the events, decisions, and losses that brought us here; the major problem is the crisis of *interpretation*, that is, the absence of shared understanding of the essentials, of what unites us, of what constitutes a foundation for each person and for all as a community.

HEARING THE STREET SWEEPER

We are told constantly that we must use all the time we have available to us, stretching every moment to the limit of its capacity. This is the way most of us live our lives, moving at a forced and frustrating pace, wishing there were more hours in a day, that we didn't need to sleep, and that the weekend would get here sooner so we can catch up on all the things we've put off doing. How often do we mutter that we need a few forty-eight-hour days or forty-day months to get everything done that we need to do? But more time is not really what we need.

Among the collateral damage of our busy lives are the things left behind, what we fail to say or do. Without realizing it, as the mountains of activity become more and more gigantic, our homes look more and more like abandoned houses, empty of real presence; the language we speak becomes incomprehensible as a language that no one speaks around us; and although we live in the same place, have the same relationships, it seems that suddenly this place is no longer our "home" and has become a kind of no-man's-land.

It takes wisdom to understand that time is not stretchable, that it is incredibly short, and that we must therefore learn to live it in the most balanced way possible. We cannot delude ourselves with the logic of compensation, convinced, for example, that we'll be able to somehow give back the time that we steal from the people we love, by organizing some event with them or buying them this or that; or that all our lost rest and contemplation can be compensated for by extravagant vacations. Both as individuals and as a society, we must learn what it means to use our time with wisdom.

In this approach to time, it is sometimes more important to know how to stop rather than how to start, more vital to pause than to make progress. I remember how, for years, in a house where I lived, I heard the street sweeper every night sweeping the fallen leaves of the hackberry tree under my window. He usually came around one in the morning. The rhythm of his broom was a reminder that it was time to wrap up my work and get to bed. Like the street sweeper gathering the dead leaves into a pile, I needed to gather the assorted pieces of my day's work and turn off the light until the next day.

Yet even this exercise of interrupting work to get some rest is not easy for many of us. It is not uncommon for this to require an exercise in detachment and poverty—to accept not having achieved all of the goals we set for ourselves; to accept that what we have achieved is only a provisional, incomplete version, full of imperfections; and to accept that we need rest and rejuvenation, because we can't attain a freshness of thought simply by willing it, and that without it, we're just turning our wheels and wasting time.

I believe the turning point happens when we look at what is left unfinished and understand it not just as a sign of one's deficiency, but as the very condition of being. To exist as a person is to inhabit, in a creative continuity, one's own incompletion and that of the world. Unfinishedness is a sign of vulnerability, but also—and I would say, above all—of openness to growth and a need for others. Each of our lives is not enough in itself. We will always need to consider the viewpoints of others who see us from a different angle, with another perspective and another state of mind. Life rarely finds meaning and completion individually, because these only come through sharing and giving.

5

LOOKING THROUGH THE OPEN DOOR OF THE PRESENT MOMENT

LOOK UP

The Lord brought Abraham outside and told him, "Look toward heaven and count the stars" (Gen 15:5). Faith is an experience of exteriority, of looking beyond our fragmented visions and perspectives. Faith calls us to "look up" as the Lord leads us outside the closed circles of our questions and our certainties. We must open the windows that overlook vast expanses, pull our eyes from the ground they have been fixed on, and contemplate the immensity inscribed in the universe and in ourselves.

Called by God to be the protagonist of a new story, Abraham lives this call as a challenge to move beyond his own context, a challenge that, because of his age, is perhaps also a challenge to time—though not even one's age, whether too old or too young, is an obstacle to the promise (see Gen 12:1). When God takes the initiative, this man, who thought he was past his time for great adventures, chooses to move beyond not only the geographical space in which his life was rooted, but also his familiar identity, surroundings, and family. Faith begins with a break, a detachment from the seemingly definitive determinisms that ground our existence, and opens us to something more, something beyond. For this reason, the journey to which God called Abraham (and calls us) demands trust. And the starting point is the call: "Look up." We must lift up our imprisoned eyes that so often seem dead to us.

THE PRISON OF THE GAZE

The text of Genesis that depicts the sin of the first human couple (see Gen 3:1–13) centers its symbolic explanation on the gaze and its limits. The serpent's promise to the woman is that "your eyes will be opened" (v. 5) and she will see with the same acuity as God. What appeals to the woman is this fiction of unlimited (and therefore inhuman) vision.

It is interesting to compare the text's depiction of the woman with its depiction of God. God simply contemplates creation: "And God saw that it was good" (1:10). God sees the goodness of each of the works of creation, considering them in their very being and not for their purpose. But the woman looks at the fruit and sees it as good because it is attractive and pleasant to the sight and to the taste: "When the woman saw that the tree was good for food, and that it was a delight to the eyes, and that the tree was to be desired to make one wise, she took of its fruit and ate; and she also gave some to her husband" (3:6).

This is the great pitfall of sight: we tend not to look at creation for itself, but for its value in relation to ourselves. We don't even realize how badly our vision is distorted by the pretension of thinking ourselves to be the measure of everything.

THE DRAMA OF THE GARDEN

The inversion of the gaze in the drama of the garden shows us that when we lose the ability to look at things for themselves, as the Creator intended, our view of the world becomes obscured. It's as if creation is withdrawn from before our eyes, with all the consequences that entails. This helps us understand better the meaning of Genesis 3:7: "Then the eyes of both were opened, and they knew that they were naked; and they sewed fig leaves together and made loincloths for themselves." This is a highly symbolic moment. When the couple realizes that they are naked, they cover their nudity, which is indicative of the difficulty they now have in looking at themselves and at their truth. Similarly, they now experience an inability to look at God. When God walks in the garden in the evening breeze, the man hides and God asks him, "Where are you?" (v. 9).

Sin imprisons our gaze; it inverts the sense of sight. Our sight becomes clouded, unable to see things in their fullness. What do we see when we see? We are far from the experience described by the poet Fernando Pessoa:

> The startling reality of things
> Is my discovery every single day.
> Every thing is what it is,
> And it's hard to explain to anyone how much this
> delights me
> And suffices me.[1]

A WORD THAT SERVES AS A MIRROR

The third chapter of Genesis offers us an ironic and vital lesson: the whole drama unfolds, not because of some extraordinary thing, but thanks to a small, seemingly unimportant object—a piece of fruit. To set creation off course in the name of a bit of fruit is completely unreasonable. Sometimes when we look at things, we miss what is most significant about them, the great meaning borne by tiny details. This is sometimes known as "the butterfly effect": the little push of the air produced by the fluttering of a butterfly's wings over the Pacific Ocean can result in a great storm in the Atlantic Ocean. The same is true in spiritual life: what is small and seemingly trivial can have great meaning.

God, a Hebrew proverb tells us, is in the details. Usually, the most obvious things completely escape us. We can scrutinize everything and everyone but are utterly unable to really see ourselves, blind to our own imperfections and vulnerability. For this we need the intervention of a third party, someone to introduce a critical viewpoint; we need to be confronted with an observation that serves as a mirror, something that is both prophetic (i.e., that leads to an honest reckoning) and poetic (that inspires and prompts us to respond).

This is what happens in the encounter between King David and the prophet Nathan. The prophet tells a parable that the king does not realize will serve as a mirror:

> The LORD sent Nathan to David. He came to him, and said to him, "There were two men in a certain city, the one rich and the other poor. The rich man had very many flocks and herds; but the poor man had nothing but one little ewe lamb, which he had bought. He brought it up, and it grew up with him and with his children; it used to eat of his meager fare, and drink from his cup, and lie in his bosom, and it was like a daughter to him. Now there came a traveler to the rich man, and he was loath to take one of his own flock or herd to prepare for the wayfarer who had come to him, but he took the poor man's lamb, and prepared that for the guest who had come to him."
> (2 Sam 12:1–4)

When David expresses his indignation over the abuse of power Nathan describes—"As the LORD lives, the man who has done this deserves to die" (v. 5)—Nathan enables him to see himself: "You are the man!" (v. 7).

I HAVE SEEN YOUR MISERY

In the Book of Exodus, the great adventure of the liberation of the people of Israel begins with the verb *to see*. God said to Moses, "I have indeed seen the misery of my people in Egypt. I have heard them crying out because of their slave drivers, and I am concerned about their suffering" (Exod 3:7, NIV). The starting point is this "I have seen." God does not close his eyes, does not turn them away from us. We need to have more trust in God's watchfulness. Our liberation begins because God sees. God sees and God's gaze is for us a promise of life, of relationship, of covenant.

COME SEE THE SUNRISE

I remember a story told to me by a close friend. Her father was a judge in Italy. He was a stern and withdrawn man who had no time to waste and little desire to turn his attention away from his important professional world, even to notice the details of his children's lives. She grew up, studied, and during the first years of her own professional life, worked as her father's secretary. This closeness did not change his relationship with her. They continued to be like two strangers, with a purely formal relationship.

She told me that one day they went on a business trip to the Greek islands. They went there by boat, a journey that involved long hours of crossing. One morning, however, she was startled by her father entering her cabin to wake her up. She looked at him without understanding what was going on. He said to her, "Come and see

the sun rising. It's huge, huge. Come quickly. You'll like it. Come."
Many years later, when her father was dead and this story was
decades old, my friend told me, "If he had only done something like
this again, only once again, I would have forgiven him everything."

THE NIGHT IS BRIGHT

Psalm 139 offers a meditation on the meaning of God's gaze
on our own existence. The love of God is not only universal; it is
also personal. I can recognize the gaze of God who knows me, who
knows how to play the singular strings of my soul, who has always
listened to my body, since I was woven into the depths of life. It is
interesting to grasp the realism of this biblical composition: "You
know when I sit down and when I rise up; / you discern my thoughts
from far away. / You search out my path and my lying down, / and
are acquainted with all my ways" (vv. 2–3).

God's gaze never ceases to bear witness to life. It is eternally
faithful, a watchful flower. We can never say, "This part of my life is
too dark or obscure for God to get involved in," because the Psalmist
says, "Even the darkness is not dark to you; / the night is as bright as
the day, / for darkness is as light to you" (v. 12).

If we believe that God looks at us with a look of love, we will
know with confidence that God's eyes go in search of ours. God does
not want to see us die. He goes down into our garden and calls to us,
asking, "Where are you?" (Gen 3:9).

LEARNING FROM THE GAZE

The Gospels teach us fundamental lessons about seeing. Think
of the Gospel of Luke and the extraordinarily visual force of what
it offers. In the Magnificat, Mary sings and we know by her song
that it is all the people of God who participate in this thanksgiving:

"My soul magnifies the Lord / ...for he has looked with favor on the lowliness of his servant" (Luke 1:46, 48). This humility is not to be understood in a moral sense. God looks upon the smallness, the baseness of his servant. God looks upon Mary, and she exalts the Lord.

In chapter 15, in the unforgettable parable of the prodigal son, when the son returns to his father's house, the role that *seeing* plays is wonderful. The text tells us, "He set off and went to his father. But while he was still far off, his father saw him and was filled with compassion; he ran and put his arms around him and kissed him" (Luke 15:20). The father's gaze is decisive in this encounter. He exceeds all expectations, even the best that the son could have hoped for this reunion. The son was planning to say, "I deserve nothing, I expect nothing. Treat me like one of your servants, because I don't deserve to be called your son." The father, however, contrary to common sense, looks upon him with love. He opens his house for the feast and offers reconciliation: "This brother of yours was dead and has come to life," he tells the reluctant older brother (Luke 15:32). This return to life follows the Father's merciful gaze upon him.

In Jesus's gaze, we find the loving gaze of the Father who goes out to meet humanity in the most improbable places, to transform our hearts. While Zacchaeus is perched in his sycamore tree, driven by a curiosity that could have stopped there, Jesus approaches him and says to him words that disconcerted everyone: "Zacchaeus, hurry and come down; for I must stay at your house today" (Luke 19:5). Would it have even occurred to Zacchaeus that this preacher would seek him on his own initiative, to welcome him? It's God's surprise. And when Zacchaeus knows that he has been seen, recognized, his life is transformed. Standing, he invites Jesus to see his transformation as well: "Look, half of my possessions, Lord, I will give to the poor; and if I have defrauded anyone of anything, I will pay back four times as much" (Luke 19:8).

CAN YOU SEE ANYTHING?

A passage from the Gospel of Mark (8:22–26) allows us to better understand the pedagogy of Jesus regarding sight:

> [Jesus and his disciples] came to Bethsaida. Some people brought a blind man to him and begged him to touch him. He took the blind man by the hand and led him out of the village; and when he had put saliva on his eyes and laid his hands on him, he asked him, "Can you see anything?" And the man looked up and said, "I can see people, but they look like trees, walking." Then Jesus laid his hands on his eyes again; and he looked intently and his sight was restored, and he saw everything clearly. Then he sent him away to his home, saying, "Do not even go into the village."

It is others, perhaps relatives or friends of this man, who approached Jesus to ask for his help. The purification of the gaze is not an individual act. Although it is a personal experience, it is not an individual act. Even if we are alone with our existential blindness, we are not without the vision we need to find our way. The experience of God's love comes to us through others, in large and small ways. We need someone to lead us to Christ so that he can reveal himself in us, showing his mercy.

Note that no one knows for sure what Jesus will do here; there is something unexpected in the air. What is fundamental is the encounter, more than the form it takes. Jesus is the protagonist; it is he who takes the initiative, even if the reason is our blindness, our difficulty in living or interpreting this moment. Christ is the agent in the experience that saves us.

Jesus takes the man by the hand and leads him outside the village. This image is one of the most extraordinary that the Gospel offers us, because it concretely translates the trust placed in Jesus.

The truth is that we could not accompany Jesus if he did not reach out to us to allow us to encounter him in privacy. We leave the village only because he takes us by the hand. But transformation only occurs when we are willing to move our usual point of view (the one we have from our village, so to speak) to a new place, which is not quite a place, but rather a relationship, an accompaniment.

The Gospel relates different kinds of moments: moments of crowds, moments when Jesus speaks only to the group of disciples or to two or three of them in particular, and moments when he speaks only to one person. The encounter can be experienced in any of these situations, but when Jesus is alone with someone, it takes on an extremely personal dimension. When he and the blind man are alone together, Jesus applies saliva to his eyes. It's a strong symbol because saliva comes from Jesus's own body. Jesus doesn't mix up a potion or offer exotic plants or fish entrails as a remedy—the remedy is Jesus himself. What transforms us is the gift that Jesus makes of himself. For this reason, the imposition of saliva is accompanied by another gesture: that of the laying on of hands, which also represents a vital transmission. It is not surprising that, in their many comments on this Gospel passage, the fathers of the church emphasized that saliva and the laying on of hands were the sacramental expression of healing.

It is significant to note that the man, up to this point, does not see where he is or where he is going; he relies on Jesus's guidance. The spiritual path involves a fundamental act of trust. We can't demand to know every step. If the sower who plants the seed digs to see if it has started to grow, he threatens the germination. The important thing is not to see or to know, but to have trust. This is how the most unexpected dialogue can take place. Jesus asks the man, "Can you see anything?" This is a specific question, not a general or abstract one. The blind man replies very simply: "I can see people, but they look like trees, walking." There is no complaint, no accusation, but the courage of objectivity: "I see this." Jesus can then correct his vision, and he will then see clearly.

When we puzzle over the "why," the "how," the "where," we fail to say what we really see. The authenticity of this man, who acknowledges, "I see badly," opens the possibility for him to be healed and to see with clarity. We need to learn this simplicity of accepting our history as it is, of accepting life without moralization, without dissimulation, without hiding things under the carpet, by exposing our poverty, trusting that Jesus can transform us.

When the man is healed, Jesus says to him, "Do not even go into the village." It is curious because Jesus had guided him out of the village, and now he tells him not even to return to it. A new horizon opens up, a new beginning for his life, and it's not about getting back to where you started, in the same place. No! Go home, begin your life again, restart your story; do not remain idle in the square, the object of everyone's curiosity. This is not what you need now. Instead, return home, build, be—live your truth as if it were a new beginning!

WHEN A LAMP GIVES YOU LIGHT WITH ITS RAYS

For Jesus, sight is crucially important, and he devoted many teachings to it. For example:

> Your eye is the lamp of your body. If your eye is healthy, your whole body is full of light; but if it is not healthy, your body is full of darkness. Therefore consider whether the light in you is not darkness. If then your whole body is full of light, with no part of it in darkness, it will be as full of light as when a lamp gives you light with its rays. (Luke 11:34–36)

How we see affects the quality of our life. Let's not imagine that we can correct the vision of others when the quality of our own vision needs attention. Impaired vision is a source of darkness. Examine the quality of the lamp that we carry: this is the challenge that Jesus offers us.

LOOK UPON THE MYSTERY OF THE CROSS

Our gaze is often like that of the disciples on the night Jesus was arrested, when he asks them to stay awake for an hour and they fall asleep (see Luke 22:45). Their sleep in the Garden of Olives is not simply the result of exhaustion from a day filled with emotions and disappointments. Rather, it represents an unwillingness to look upon the mystery of the cross. This unwillingness prompts us to close our own eyes, too. The pedagogy of Jesus that we discover in the Gospel converts our sight and allows us gradually to move to a deeper level of understanding. "If any want to become my followers, let them deny themselves and take up their cross daily and follow me" (Luke 9:23).

THE EYE DOCTOR

Jesus's dialogue with the woman at the well begins with a succession of misunderstandings. First: "How is it that you, a Jew, ask a drink of me, a woman of Samaria?" (John 4:9). Shortly after: "Sir, you have no bucket, and the well is deep. Where do you get that living water?" (John 4:11). The shift occurs when she perceives, through conversation with him about her own life, that Jesus is not taken in by deceptive superficial appearances, but that he sees within her. This is when the transformation takes place. This woman, at first reluctant, runs to the village to say, "Come and see a man who told me everything I have ever done! He cannot be the Messiah, can he?" (John 4:29). Christ is the "eye doctor." He opens a path for us to move from seeing to contemplating, from the simple look to the look of faith.

AT THE HEART OF WEAKNESS

It is our nakedness, our misery, our misfortune, our blindness that put us on the path to Jesus. Because this man is blind and because he knows that he is blind, Jesus asks him, "What do you want me to do for you?" (Mark 10:51).

We often think of holiness as the alternative to sin or weakness. If that's the case, we conclude, then it's the opposite of my life. But in fact, we don't find holiness apart from weakness or temptation, but at the very heart of weakness and temptation. We don't begin to become holy only after we've managed to overcome our weakness; on the contrary, even when we are weak, we are close to holiness. Holiness transforms every moment, however difficult, into opportunities. This is what the psalm reminds us: "Hear, O daughter, consider and incline your ear; / forget your people and your father's house, / and the king will desire your beauty" (Ps 45:10–11).

Even if we find ourselves in extreme misery, God is in love with our beauty. So, from the depths of your night, fix your eyes upon the glow of a star.

ASSUMING I'M THE ONE WHO CAN'T SEE WELL

Jesus offered the following parable:

Can a blind person guide a blind person? Will not both fall into a pit? A disciple is not above the teacher, but everyone who is fully qualified will be like the teacher. Why do you see the speck in your neighbor's eye, but do not notice the log in your own eye? Or how can you say to your neighbor, 'Friend, let me take out the speck in your eye,' when you yourself do not see the log in your own eye? You hypocrite, first take the log out of your own eye, and then you will see clearly to take the speck out of your neighbor's eye. (Luke 6:39–42)

We are quick to detect faults in the eyes of others, to find weaknesses, to notice impediments, but that's not the path to transformation.

When obstacles obscure our vision, though we think we see, we are incapable of doing so. What heals us is to acknowledge the "beam" in our eye, the imperfection that affects our vision. What changes us is to accept that the problem is ours and not that of others. How many relational crises, how many conflicts plunge us into suffering to the point that we realize that we have an interior path to take? Sometimes, at first, we can only say, "How could this have happened to me? How could all of this have befallen me, after all I did?" Often our first attitude is to consider ourselves to be a victim. It is others who have a beam in their eyes and who do not see. Then we gradually enter a path of growth, and we begin to accept that perhaps the problem lies not solely with others, but with ourselves. This change is essential—to get out of the mode of victim, to stop spreading bitterness, and to assume the problem to be our own. It's the only way to life. Only then will our sight return to clarity instead of hanging on to pain and resentment indefinitely.

There is no mature spiritual life without the capacity to look life in the face, with vision that integrates both what has been good and what has gone wrong, to make everything an occasion of praise and thanksgiving, so that we can pray, "Lord, I give you thanks for the road traveled, for the way it has been traveled. I thank you for my story, for the falling illusions because I ended up seeing the beam that was in my eye. Thank you for my path of conversion and acceptance. Healing is only given to me when I recognize that I need to be healed, to go further, to live more fully."

When we throw a pebble and it bounces, it can go farther than we expected. The truth is that the opportunities to bounce in our life are opportunities to experience compassion, growth, and forgiveness.

Therefore, let there be no mistake: our real problem is not someone else or some other thing. It's more than that. Our problem has to do with the meaning of all things. Our problem is with God. This is where we need to focus our energy.

There is a story about two monks who go on a trip. On the bank of a river, they meet a woman who asks if she can climb on the back of one of them to get safely to the other bank. One of them immediately offers to carry the woman to the other side. They cross the river, and he puts her back onto the ground. After they say goodbye and the woman goes on her way, the other monk begins to lecture him saying, "You're a monk. You should never have touched that woman." He went on admonishing his companion like this for miles as they walked along their way, asking how he could have done such a thing, until the other monk finally said, "I carried that woman from one bank of the river to the other and then put her down. You've continued to drag her along ever since."

How often we drag unimportant questions way beyond reason; for years and years, we struggle under their burdens and illusions, only because our gaze has not yet been converted.

The Gospel of John is often called the gospel of faith because it reveals so much about the nature of faith. But in this text, faith is not a static thing. Rather, it is a dynamism, a movement toward the person of Jesus; it is to believe in Jesus and to confess that he is the Son of God. The Gospel of John is the gospel of faith because it is also the gospel of vision. However, in this narrative where faith in fact occupies a central place, there is a shadow, seen from the start: it is the shadow of unbelief. Despite Jesus's revelation of himself, despite his power and the signs that he fulfilled, we find an inability to see that traps hearts and leads them to disbelief.

"The true light, which enlightens everyone, was coming into the world. He was in the world, and the world came into being through him; yet the world did not know him. He came to what was his own, and his own people did not accept him" (John 1:9–11). It's all in the opposition expressed in those two possessives: he came to his own, and his own did not accept him. But like the serpent that Moses raised in the wilderness, we will look upon the one who was lifted up, and he will heal our hearts. Faith is a great school of vision.

OPEN YOUR EYES

"Do not worry about your life" (Luke 12:22), Jesus tells us. It seems to be the most paradoxical and most unexpected thing we can hear, because our lives are full of anxiety. It is the great motive of our existence. And now Jesus comes to tell us, "Don't worry."

It sometimes seems like the only thing we can do well is worry about our lives. It prevents us from creating, making plans, smiling and being truly present to other people, taking a walk without a destination in mind, and even praying. We monitor our accounts and seek greater security. We feel the weight of life, so many concerns weighing upon us.

So why does Jesus say, "Don't worry"? He explains, "Life is more than food, and the body more than clothing" (Luke 12:23). The Lord tells us this: Your life is worth more than your house, your work, your prospects for change, more than the things that pile up. Life is more than that. If we do not perceive this saving truth, then we burn the vitality and the promise of our existence; we exhaust our forces in a useless struggle. When we understand that life is more than that, we stop being so worried about insignificant things, being trapped in ridiculous trifles that enslave us. We are like ants in a quarry, managing small grains as if they were everything.

Jesus's proposition is simple: open your eyes. "Consider the ravens: they neither sow nor reap, they have neither storehouse nor barn, and yet God feeds them. Of how much more value are you than the birds!...Consider the lilies, how they grow: they neither toil nor spin; yet I tell you, even Solomon in all his glory was not clothed like one of these" (Luke 12:24, 27).

Opening your eyes to more of life is important. It's also exceedingly rare. We have our eyes closed, and we only see what we want to see. However, it is necessary to open our eyes in order that fear can give way to joy. We suffocate in these tight lives that we construct for ourselves. But there is no point in living unhappily. Good heavens! Life is worth more than that.

Let us therefore notice what Jesus's pedagogy consists of: *Look at the ravens. Look at the lilies.* What he says and what he doesn't say reveals who Jesus is and what is important to him. He doesn't say, "Consider the richest person. Consider the one who has done best." Not even "Consider the smartest person." No, Jesus points us to the gratuitous beauty that proceeds from being. A bird cannot put on a hat, and a lily cannot dress up its petals. The bird does not gather, nor does the lily have a wardrobe. They are only what they are, and they live it fully. In the same way, our lives are not about gathering toys for ourselves, but of discovering what resides in us.

We load our lives with things—some are essentials, but others (most, in fact) are superfluous, and they become a net that entangles us. We build up lives that are stable and secure, but that's an illusion because we have mortgaged our fundamental truth in exchange for all our concerns. Part of our problems are these vicious circles that we set up and that are so many invisible prisons that our freedom collapses. We want to control everything, and we say, "My life is going to be like this, my life has to be like this." As a result, we lose our freedom. Because life is not like what we have in mind, and it can't be. Why not understand, then, the paradoxical path of life? It's when I *give* my life and from my life that my life multiplies.

Our great temptation is to ask, "Father, give me this, Father, give me that," when the most important thing is to trust and to give, to hand over what we are. These two attitudes are reflected in the parable of the prodigal son: the attitude that says, "Father, give me the share of the property that will belong to me" (Luke 15:12) and the one that abandons any claim, saying, "Father, I have sinned against heaven and before you; I am no longer worthy to be called your son" (Luke 15:21). This is where the Father answers, "This son of mine was dead and is alive again" (Luke 15:24).

Jesus's "Do not worry about your life" is another way of saying "Hand over your life." This is a decisive element in our configuration to Jesus.

Spirituality is no longer a priority for many. We may think we're putting some effort into being religious people, but that doesn't mean much; spirituality is not one of our concerns, nor even the main one. The real mystic is the one who lives with abandon.

TO BE ABLE TO SEE MYSELF

It is interesting to find, in another of the Johannine texts, the passage from the Book of Revelation where Christ addresses the churches in Asia. Christ is the one who transmits knowledge and gives us sight. This is how he addresses the church in Laodicea:

I know your works; you are neither cold nor hot. I wish that you were either cold or hot. So, because you are luke-warm, and neither cold nor hot, I am about to spit you out of my mouth. For you say, 'I am rich, I have prospered, and I need nothing.' You do not realize that you are wretched, pitiable, poor, blind, and naked. Therefore I counsel you to buy from me gold refined by fire so that you may be rich; and white robes to clothe you and to keep the shame of your nakedness from being seen; and salve to anoint your eyes so that you may see. (Rev 3:15–18)

We need eye drops—Jesus himself—to restore our sight. We must look into our own depths and understand that self-sufficiency is an illusion, that our situation is one of weakness, deficiency, and imperfection. Isaac the Syrian said,

> Blessed is the man who knows his own weakness. Blessed is he who says, "I am miserable, I am miserable, I am poor, I am blind, I am mute." He who knows his sin is greater than he who raises the dead by his prayer. He who weeps for an hour over his own sin is greater than he who is at the service of the entire world. He who has been judged worthy to see himself as he is is greater than he who has been given to see the angels.

More important than being able to contemplate the angels is to be able to see myself, as I am, because it is only on this condition that Jesus can act.

LOOKING AT THE WORLD WITH GOD'S EYES

As a young woman, the philosopher Simone Weil felt that, to understand the lives of the working class, she could not be content to teach philosophy; she wanted a concrete experience of the life of workers. So she quit her teaching job and worked for nearly a year first in one and then in another car factory.

This was a radical experience for her. First, she had to deal with her physical frailty and the constant, demanding physical activity involved in the work. As one might expect, this made her daily life difficult, but her greatest suffering was spiritual. Her original intention had been to consider how workers could make their work the subject of reflection and contemplation. But she soon discovered that the nature of work prevented this from happening, because the main duty, by the yardstick of which every worker was rewarded or punished, was speed of production. This made the experience of work monotonous, mechanical, and dehumanizing. Simone wrote,

> The effect of exhaustion is to make me forget my real reasons for spending time in the factory, and to make it almost impossible for me to overcome the strongest temptation that this life entails: that of not thinking anymore, which is the one and only way of not suffering from it. It's only on Saturday afternoon and Sunday that a few memories and shreds of ideas return to me, and I remember that I am *also* a thinking being.[2]

When the only thing that matters is that a person can function mechanically, like a gear in a machine, then what follows, sooner or later, is the destruction of personhood. This is what Simone testifies to.

The Bible talks often about human work and associates it with God's own work. The first chapter of Genesis shows us a God who works diligently over the period of a week. It is important to observe that God's work is only completed when, having completed the work of creation, God contemplates it in its original goodness and sees that everything is good (or very good). Simone Weil wanted each person's work to be for them an object of contemplation. It is not without reason that the text that inaugurates biblical revelation is a kind of hymn to the gaze. God confirms and reveals, not only by his action, but also by his gaze, the intrinsic goodness of creation.

Biblical studies have helped us to perceive the role played in this text by *separation*: God creates by separating. God separates the waters that are below the firmament from the waters that are above. God distinguishes the different lights, creates individualities, existences, and various missions. From this separation also arises the possibility of God *uncovering*, removing the veil that covers the goodness or the beauty of each creature. Thus, behind all that is created is God's gaze of love, God's gaze of admiration without instrumentalization, with no other end than that of announcing fullness.

We might try the following spiritual exercise: to look at creation—at ourselves and at the world—as though with the wondrous gaze of God. Isak Dinesen (the pseudonym of Danish author Karen Blixen) describes such a viewpoint beautifully in her novel *Out of Africa*:

> You have tremendous views as you get up above the African highlands, surprising combinations and changes of light and coloring, the rainbow on the green sunlit land, the gigantic upright clouds and big wild black storms, all swing round you in a race and a dance. The lashing hard showers of rain whiten the air askance. The language is short of words for the experiences of flying, and will have to invent new words with time....You may at other times fly low enough to see the animals on the plains and to feel towards them as God did when he had just created them.[3]

EYES HAVE TWO FUNCTIONS

"The eyes are remarkable creations!" exclaimed Antonio Vieira, a seventeenth-century Portuguese Jesuit, in his preaching. "All of humanity's senses have only one purpose; only the eyes have two. The ears hear, the tongue tastes, the nose smells, the hands feel; only the eyes have two purposes: to see and to cry."[4] The tears that our eyes shed are very personal. They are an intimate revelation of ourselves, of what makes us sad or happy or hurt. The way we cry and the reasons we cry expose us: "Through my tears, I tell a story," writes the French author Roland Barthes.[5]

In the Gospels, we see Jesus cry over the death of a friend (John 11:35) and the fate of a city (Luke 19:41). Peter weeps for Jesus (Matt 26:75), and so do the women who watch him carry his cross (Luke 23:28). On one occasion, a woman whose name we never learn bursts into a meal where Jesus is present and carries out with her tears a ritual of hospitality that had been denied to him (Luke 7:36–50).

Crying has a place in Christian spirituality. Tears are the mark of what Origen called "sorrow according to God," which is not, he said, a voluntary sadness but "a permanent sorrow caused by the sorrow over sin," a thirst of the soul, a spiritual silence in which moisture comes to refresh the burn of the lack of God. There is even a whole devotional literature regarding the "gift of tears." The philosopher Emil Cioran once said that tears are what allow someone to become a saint after being a person.

CONTEMPLATION BEGINS WITH THE ACCEPTANCE OF BEING UNABLE TO SEE

Contemplation begins when we accept that we cannot see that our vision is partial and poor, that "we see in a mirror, dimly" (1 Cor 13:12). Contemplation is not a wisdom we attain; it is rather a form of standing disarmed before God's gaze without reserve and learning to do it again and again. Simone Weil said we only contemplate an apple when we do not intend to eat it. This is the surrender capable of releasing wonder.

ACCESS TO THE DEPTH OF LIFE

Millions of readers probably are unaware, but the place where *The Little Prince* was most likely born is a hospital bed in New York, where Antoine de Saint-Exupéry was being treated following an accident in 1941. A friend had given him a box of watercolors. In the no-man's-land of his American exile, a prisoner of the loneliness of his long hospital stay, he sketched the parable of the child traveler in love with his rose. Saint-Exupéry knew only too well the spiritual uprooting of the modern world, which prefers to consume rather than to be consumed with love; he knew the widening gap between technology and humanity, the accumulation of knowledge and the scarcity of wisdom. His plan was to lead the reader to the outer desert, to make us aware of the inner desertification that takes hold of everything and that in this way, we revive in ourselves thirst and desire.

It is common to associate *The Little Prince* with a joyful but naive vision of life. But when we venture to reread it carefully, this impression doesn't fade but becomes more complex, nuanced, and realistic. Uniting sorrow and joy in the same vision of existence, linking patience and tears in the same vision, understanding that the darkest night and the lightness of laughter are sewn of the same thread are lessons that give us access to the depth of life.

MIRROR, MIRROR

Consider the story of Snow White. The stepmother who continually looks in the mirror asking, "Mirror, mirror on the wall, who's the fairest of them all?" illustrates our way of seeing. Our gaze is always preoccupied with ourselves, and we fill life with mirrors that only confirm our illusions of power or self-sufficiency.

We forget, however, that mirrors reflect two-dimensional images, without the depth that comes from looking within ourselves. We deceive ourselves by judging that the mirrors that surround us reflect reality, when in fact what we see in them is only part of reality, a part that is not without ambiguity. How does the transformation of the gaze work in us? This is what we should ask ourselves, remembering the words of Marcel Proust: "The real voyage of discovery consists not in seeking new landscapes, but in having new eyes."[6]

CÉZANNE'S APPLES

An artist is a master of the gaze. This is how I like to think of the nineteenth-century French painter Paul Cézanne. His entire career was about revealing a fascinating visual aspect of the world, always searching—in each landscape, each character, every ordinary apple—for something we never completely reach. Cézanne explained it like this: "What I am trying to translate to you is more mysterious; it is entwined in the very roots of being, in the implacable source of sensations."

He constantly painted the same objects, and he painted them for themselves, for their spiritual resonance. His technique was the layering of successive colors without mixing them. To achieve this effect, he had to wait until the first layer was dry before applying the next—an extraordinarily slow, rigorous, and *contemplative* process. He concentrated on color and, through this technique, synthesized his experience of revelation and awareness of things. "The mountain thinks of me and I become its conscience"—this was his leitmotif. For this reason, whoever said that "suspended between nature and utility, [Cézanne's apples] only exist to be contemplated" was not mistaken. These apples that could simply be on our table are a kind of exercise for the eye. These small spheres, light and compact, that take shape under the play of light, illuminate our unstable ability to grasp what is dark.

THE PLEASURE OF WAITING

I love a story about Frederico Fellini told by Tonino Guerra. The great filmmaker used to arrive early to all his appointments, whether it was a business meeting or a meal with friends. He arrived on the scene and passed the time, wandering here and there with pleasure, without alerting anyone to his arrival. When a friend realized this and asked him why he hadn't immediately knocked on the door, his response was that he wanted to *enjoy the pleasure of waiting*.

Our society has naively elevated efficiency and utility to mythical levels; it sees no value in waiting. In the tight deadlines we impose on ourselves, we can only see waiting as an irritating, old-fashioned, and obsolete problem. Why wait? From ready-to-wear clothes to cooked meals, from real-time communication to instant results— waiting has become a dead weight that we do not know what to do with and that we must throw overboard.

Maybe this desire for immediacy is a defensive reflex against a growing fear that at the end of this fast-paced life, there is ultimately no one and nothing to hope for. When everyone lives under high pressure, everything becomes dangerously precarious. We are aware of this, but we keep it to ourselves. We're afraid to talk about it.

We're hypermodern, versatile people, equipped with a wide array of technologies to make tasks quicker and easier, and yet we remain dependent, insecure, and dissatisfied. We live through experiences without ever internalizing them, on the verge of exhaustion and disengaged from creation. We need to understand that waiting is not necessarily a waste of time. It is often the opposite. To wait is to become aware of one's time, of the time necessary to be. It means taking time for yourself, for maturation, for growth. It is to perceive that time is not just a framework, but that it has meaning in itself. Someone who, for example, insists on immediately satisfying every desire will have a hard time understanding what desire *is*—or, at least, what great desire is. One who does not wait patiently after planting a seed will never have the joy of watching it bloom.

SEEING THE CREATURES

One of the most moving texts I have ever read is a letter from the Polish philosopher and trade unionist Rosa Luxemburg. She wrote it from the Breslau women's prison, a few months before her execution, to one of her friends at Christmastime in 1917. As the paradoxical year ended, few dared to predict with confidence what the world of the time was rushing to. Rosa Luxemburg's text remains explicitly engaged in this historical context, defending the revolution underway in Russia against the perspectives presented by the "correspondents of the bourgeois newspapers" who described this situation as an outburst of madness. Admittedly, this is the most dated and biased aspect of her letter. Luxemburg was a visionary about Germany, seeing, for example, the possibility of a pogrom, but she did not have the same foresight about Russia.

Yet there are passages that prompted the writer Karl Kraus to call this letter "a document of humanity and poetry" that should be taught to future generations. Luxemburg talks about the third Christmas she was spending in prison. She is looking for a Christmas tree, but all she can find is a miserable and bare shrub, which she still takes to her cell. This pushes her to wonder about the "joyful intoxication" that she maintained in the heart of this hell, this kind of irreducible trust that persisted within her, despite the discomfort and desolation. That night she wrote,

> I lie here alone and in silence, enveloped in the manifold black wrappings of darkness, tedium, unfreedom, and winter—and yet my heart beats with an immeasurable and incomprehensible inner joy, just as if I were moving in the brilliant sunshine across a flowery mead....At such moments I think of you, and would that I could hand over this magic key to you also. Then, at all times and in all places, you would be able to see the beauty, and the joy of life.[7]

When she wonders about the cause of the joy she feels, she concludes that "there is no cause," and she writes, "I believe that the key to the riddle is simply life itself."[8]

The last part of the letter is equally unforgettable. Luxemburg describes the arrival at the prison of wagons full of food, drawn by buffalos captured in Romania. For the first time, she notices the unspeakable suffering of these animals, which were being "unmercifully flogged" by the wagon drivers. It is both a shock and a revelation to her. When she dares to ask a wagon driver "if he had no compassion" for these exhausted creatures, he responded with what Luxemburg called "an evil smile," saying, "No more than anyone has compassion for us men," striking the buffalos even more violently.[9]

Luxembourg then writes how her gaze then fixed on one of them. The animal was bleeding, its hide torn, but it stood motionless, looking at her with an expression in its eyes

> like that of a weeping child—one that has been severely thrashed and does not know why, nor how to escape from the torment of ill-treatment. I stood in front of the team; the beast looked at me; the tears welled from my own eyes. The suffering of a dearly loved brother could hardly have moved me more profoundly than I was moved by my impotence in the face of this mute agony.[10]

Out of this empathy, which now linked this woman to an anonymous wounded animal, was born a new form of resistance to brutality and barbarism. In this vision of "the splendor of war,"[11] Rosa Luxembourg understood that communion between people and other creatures was not only possible, but urgent and necessary.

DEVELOPING ATTENTION

We have all had the experience of spending time in school studying incomprehensible things and filling our notebooks with indecipherable formulas, useless dates, or outdated concepts. What will all this have been for? I don't want to discourage anyone, but

Kant said that one of the benefits of school is that people learn to sit. Not much, right?

One of the most extraordinary texts by Simone Weil is an essay she called "Reflections on the Right Use of School Studies with a View to the Love of God." It shows that the dryness of so many exercises—in Latin or geometry, for example—useless as they sometimes seem to be, from a certain point of view, make of us, without our realizing it, travelers worthy of the name. Each school exercise, however meaningless it may seem to us, is a special way of yearning for the truth. Here is how Weil puts it:

> If we concentrate our attention on trying to solve a problem of geometry, and if at the end of an hour we are no nearer to doing so than at the beginning, we have nevertheless been making progress each minute of that hour in another more mysterious dimension. Without our knowing or feeling it, this apparently barren effort has brought more light into the soul.[12]

She is telling us that living our lives well requires of us a way of looking at things that looks for more than what is immediately useful, but which is open to gratuitousness, to what we do for reasons that we may not know, and that only the future can make clear.

AT EVERY MOMENT, WE RELEARN

I find Merleau-Ponty's explanation of *attention* especially useful. According to him, attention is not, strictly speaking, an association of images or matching one's thought to the object that one seeks to grasp. Attention is about *relearning* how to look at an object.[13]

What does this say to us who use our knowledge of yesterday to judge the moment of today?

LOOK AT EVERYTHING AS IF FOR THE FIRST TIME

The best definition of the traveler that I know comes from the French writer Jacques Lacarrière: "The real traveler is one who, at each new place, begins again the adventure of life."

I firmly believe that what we are really doing when we travel is, consciously or not, trying to reconstruct ourselves, even if the experience of travel in our consumer society has become quick, streamlined, predictable, and closer to a euphoric escape than an exploration. Despite all that, encountering borders around us always sends us back to our interior borders, and it will always be so. Inevitably, geography tends to become metaphorical, and there is no traveler in this world who does not realize, sooner or later, with joy or sorrow, that the most important journey is the one we make within ourselves. "Bitter knowledge, that we gain by travelling!" wrote the poet Charles Baudelaire with his characteristic pessimism. But even this bitter knowledge is necessary, in proper proportion, in order to weave the incomplete interiority that we are.

Anyone who thinks that travel is only an external experience should think again. We don't just walk the topography of a landscape. Moving, whether we realize it or not, means changing positions, approaching things from a new angle, exposing ourselves to diversity. This requires a maturation of the gaze itself, the recognition that we are missing something, the adaptation to other realities, other times, other languages, or at least the realization that we are incapable of it. It is a confrontation from which we cannot escape, a difficult dialogue that necessarily obliges us to do further work on ourselves. The experience of travel is an experience of borders and openness, both of which each person needs to exist. It can express a state of mind, constitute a symptom, revive flagging spirits, or establish a break with one's past. In this multiplicity of possible meanings,

151

the journey appears as a fundamental interpretation device. At the same time, it is a window and a mirror.

It is our consciousness that travels, that discovers every detail of the world and looks at everything with a fresh eye, as if for the first time. Travel can prompt this new vision. It is an optical lens. It is an observatory erected above a flat life. For this reason, travel can introduce into our routine existence elements that will bring about a recontextualization, a moment of rebirth.

WHAT DID I SEE?

Very often, in the evening of life, we are beset by the temptation to believe that we've done everything but built nothing, that our life has not even laid a foundation. We look at our hands and they are empty, bare, and the temptation is to ask, "Was it worth it? Have I really lived? What did I listen to? What did my eyes see?"

BEGGARS LOOKING AT THE MOON

Happiness is not something we spend a lot of time consciously thinking about, but we need to. The writer Milan Kundera said there is only one important question to ask: Why are we not happy? We know it, but we do everything to get as far away from conversations like this as possible. We prefer to leave our happiness up to chance or superstition, as if it depended on the capricious whims of fate rather than being our own responsibility.

We tend to look at happiness like beggars look at the moon— without knowing very well what to think of it, accepting that it may not be of this world, but marveling at its loveliness. To accept that happiness demands learning, knowledge, or skill is a step that we are reluctant to take. This reluctance is certainly, to a large extent, cultural. Our societies, which place a blissful confidence in everything that relates to technology and everything that comes from it, practice a militant agnosticism regarding the ability of each person to be happy. About happiness, it seems like we have nothing to say to each other. About well-being, sure. About prosperity, which we idolize, certainly, but not happiness.

We don't even realize that, in the dance between the generations, there is a big void: we don't know if our parents or our children are happy. We never even ask one another about it.

THE COLOR THAT WASN'T

Blue has long been a nearly invisible color in the West. There was a time when it was, both in social life and in artistic creation, virtually unknown. In the first century, the Roman writer Pliny the Elder referred to a four-color palette that the best artists use—none of the four is blue. We know the Egyptians discreetly applied blue on their funerary works of art and that, for them and other peoples of the ancient East, blue was perceived as a beneficial color, almost an amulet to repel the forces of evil. But this idea did not make its way to the Romans, who considered it an Eastern (which meant "barbarian") concept. Bright blue was seen as tasteless and uncouth, and dark blue was inferior, pessimistic, and disturbing. In Rome, dressing in blue was looked upon as a breach of etiquette or a sign of mourning; having blue eyes was a kind of biological accident that evoked pity.

But after the year 1000, blue was rehabilitated and its status changed. This shift was brought about thanks to its use in representations of the Virgin Mary. Gradually, it rose in dignity, in brightness, becoming soft and luminous, positive and festive. The extraordinary development of devotion to Mary popularized blue in other fields. Kings began to dress in blue—and not just legendary kings like King Arthur (who was almost always depicted wearing blue). Imitating them, this was followed by the nobility. Like black, blue took on a moral connotation—it was the color of honesty and temperance, of heaven and of the Spirit. In just a few centuries, it achieved the status of a preferred and ubiquitous color. Blue was the color of young Werther, the protagonist of the novel published by Goethe in 1774; he drew behind him a multitude of imitators all over Europe. The flower of Novalis was blue, establishing it as one of the most ambitious and enduring symbols of the Romantic movement. The military uniforms of the new regime established by the French Revolution were blue. So were the jeans that Levi Strauss marketed in the 1860s, used first as clothing for workers and then for everyone else.

If we ask a child today what color the sky is, they will most likely answer, "blue." But it has not always been so. Undisputed masters of Western thought, such as Aristotle, Lucretia, or Seneca, said that the sky was red, yellow, purple, green, or orange. This is how they observed it, applying the analytical rigor for which we know them. This only thickens the mystery. None of them observed what seems obvious to us. This observation led the historian of colors Michel Pastoureau to wonder whether the people of antiquity were able to "see" blue, or whether they saw it as well as we see it. One thing seems certain: colors are not only natural phenomena; they are also the result of a complex human and cultural construction. The blue that was before Aristotle's eyes, and that he did not recognize, should prompt us to wonder what might be before our own eyes without us realizing it. It might plant in us a humble question: what color, that we cannot see, is the sky?

LOOKING TO THE FUTURE WITHOUT FEAR

A great historian José Mattoso says that history itself shows that action is not enough; contemplation is also necessary, perhaps even

more than action, and without contemplation, action is worthless. Despite everything, contemplation is a demanding practice. It requires choices that we are no longer used to: meditation, self-giving, silence, creative solitude. It demands from those who embrace it a real decentering of the self that is not always easy, but Mattoso rightly states that "as long as there are human beings who engage, body and soul, in contemplation, we can look to the future without fear."

TEMPTED BY THE CLOUD-MOVING WIND

In the spring of 1689, the poet Matsuo Basho set out on his longest journey. He would then have been around forty-five years old, so he was not exactly a young man on his first adventure. It is estimated that he covered more than 2,500 kilometers on foot during the two and a half years of his journey. In the prologue to the journal he kept, he wrote,

> Days and months are travelers of eternity. So are the years that pass by. Those who steer a boat across the sea, or drive a horse over the earth till they succumb to the weight of years, spend every minute of their lives travelling. There are a great number of ancients, too, who died on the road. I myself have been tempted for a long time by the cloud-moving wind—filled with a strong desire to wander.[14]

CONCLUSION

At the end of this journey that we have traveled together, dear reader, my greatest wish is that we agree on this: the key to understanding mysticism, and in particular a mysticism of the present moment, is the word *relationship*. Before even considering any specific religious heritage, we must grasp the anthropological structure that makes up each of us. The key is this: we are made in the image and likeness of God.

At the root of our being, in the depths of what we are, is a fundamental experience that absolutely takes us away from loneliness or self-sufficiency: none of us is our own origin. As scholasticism teaches, the human person is not *ens causa sui*. We don't create ourselves, neither in our beginning, nor our present, nor our future. We come from a horizon and circumstances that transcend us. It is true that we are always able to fashion in our own way what we receive from the Other, but our interiority, our very intimacy, our journey are always organized in a necessary and creative encounter with the "you." Mysticism is this covenant, always to be reinvented, between the human "I" and the divine "you."

How do we define this covenant? We find a good example of this in language. Today, two theories on the origin of language are common; indeed, they are almost taken for granted. One is the "communicative" theory. This maintains that we speak to *communicate*, to *convey* our thoughts from one head to another. The other is the "cognitive" theory. It suggests that we speak to *think*, to *develop*

our own thoughts. Both theories view language as a mental reality, that is, something that is more about thought than the body, more a transfer of reasoning than an exchange of emotions.

However, the anthropologist Dean Falk, in a fascinating book called *Finding Our Tongues*,[1] suggests something quite different. He proposes that when each of us begins to use linguistic sounds, we do it not primarily to communicate or to think, but first to *maintain contact* with those who care for us. Words are the verbalization of the desire we have for others. Basically, whatever we want to say, we say it to bring the other closer to us or hold her by our side, to delay her absence or restore her presence, to express how much she means to us. For this reason, human language is a spectacular consequence of our need for relationships.

The mysticism of everyday life, then, is nothing if not this: the unfinished and fragile construction of relationships in our life. In the mystical experience, God passes from the third to the second person: God ceases to be a "he" or "she" or "this" and becomes for us a *"you."* God ceases to be indefinite and acquires the proximity of a face, the splendor of a person.

All liturgical traditions tell us this: mysticism is practiced only by way of the body. The liturgy is intensely corporeal. The sacraments require a material (the water of baptism, the oil of confirmation, the bread and wine of the Eucharist, etc.). The spiritual supposes the sensible. This explains why the spiritual ecstasies of St. Teresa are rooted in her body—as Bernini's magnificent statue makes so clear—and the contemplation of St. Francis of Assisi made him levitate three meters above of the ground but also in another way to stay profoundly grounded, with a prophetic audacity, an expansive love.

Religion without the body is sad, incomprehensible, and disembodied, because it is with the body that we love God. It is the body that opens us, like a window, to transcendence. The experience of God is lived from the body and in connection with the body. Wouldn't the future of Christianity take this path?

NOTES

PART ONE:
A SPIRITUALITY
FOR OUR TIME

1. Augustine, *De vera religione* 39, 72.

2. Louis-Marie Chauvet, *Symbol and Sacrament: Sacramental Reinterpretation of Christian Existence*, trans. Madeleine M. Beaumont and Patrick Madigan, SJ (Collegeville, MN: Liturgical Press, 1994), 146.

3. Friedrich Nietzsche, *Thus Spoke Zarathustra*, trans. R. J. Hollingdale (New York: Penguin, 1961), 62.

4. Karl Rahner, *Theological Investigations*, vol. 5: *Later Writings*, trans. Karl-H. Kruger (London: Darton, Longman & Todd, 1966), 7.

5. Etty Hillesum, *Etty: The Letters and Diaries of Etty Hillesum, 1941–1943*, ed. Klass A. D. Smelick, trans. Arnold J. Pomerans (Ottawa: Novalis, 2002), 386.

6. Fernando Pessoa, "I Am Tired," in *Selected Poems*, 2nd ed., trans. Jonathan Griffin (New York: Penguin, 1982), 128.

7. Fernando Pessoa, *The Book of Disquiet*, trans. Alfred MacAdam (New York: Pantheon Books, 1991).

8. Fernando Pessoa, "Maritime Ode," in *Poems of Fernando Pessoa*, trans. Edwin Honig and Susan M. Brown (San Francisco: City Lights, 1986), 68.

9. René Crevel, *My Body and I*, trans. Robert Bononno (Brooklyn: Archipelago Books, 2005).

10. Virginia Wolff, *The Waves* (New York: Harcourt, 1931), 7.

11. Rainer Maria Rilke, *Auguste Rodin*, trans. Jessie Lemont and Hans Trausil (Los Angeles: The J. Paul Getty Museum, 2018; orig. ed. 1919), 47.

12. Jean-Jacques Rousseau, *Émile: Or, Concerning Education*, trans. Eleanor Worthington (Boston: D. C. Heath, 1889), 110.

13. See Richard Wrangham, *Catching Fire: How Cooking Made Us Human* (New York: Basic Books, 2009).

14. [Translator's note: In the French, the words *knowledge* and *flavor* are very similar: *savoir* and *saveur*.]

15. Pope Francis, apostolic exhortation *Evangelii Gaudium* (November 24, 2013), no. 24.

16. Walter Benjamin, *Illuminations*, trans. Harry Zohn (New York: Schocken, 1968), 184.

17. Clarice Lispector, *Água Viva*, trans. Stefan Tobler (New York: New Directions, 2012), 23.

18. Maurice Merleau-Ponty, "Eye and Mind," trans. Carleton Dallery, in *The Primacy of Perception*, ed. James M. Edie (Evanston, IL: Northwestern University Press, 1964), 162.

19. Nicholas of Cusa, *On the Vision of God, in Selected Spiritual Writings*, trans. H. Lawrence Bond (New York: Paulist, 1997), nn. 30, 40 (pp. 249, 253).

20. Susan Sontag, "The Aesthetics of Silence," in *Styles of Radical Will* (New York: Picador, 2002; orig. ed. 1966), 3.

21. Dietrich Bonhoeffer, *Letters and Papers from Prison*, Dietrich Bonhoeffer Works vol. 8, trans. Isabel Best et al. (Minneapolis: Fortress Press, 2009), 480.

22. Abraham Joshua Heschel, *The Sabbath: Its Meaning for Modern Man* (New York: Farrar, Straus and Giroux, 1951), 10.

23. Michel de Certeau, *The Mystic Fable*, vol. 1: *The Sixteenth and Seventeenth Centuries*, trans. Michael B. Smith (Chicago: University of Chicago Press, 1992), 299.

24. Certeau, *Mystic Fable*, 299.

25. Romain Rolland to Sigmund Freud, December 5, 1927, in William B. Parsons, *The Enigma of the Oceanic Feeling: Revisioning the Psychoanalytic Theory of Mysticism*, "Appendix: The Letters of Sigmund Freud and Romain Rolland" (New York: Oxford University Press, 1999), 173–74.

26. Sigmund Freud to Roman Rolland, July 20, 1929, in Parsons, *Enigma of Oceanic Feeling*, 175.

27. Michel de Certeau, *Le voyage mystique* (Paris: Cerf, 1988), 27.

28. Pessoa, *Book of Disquiet*.

29. Karl Rahner, "The Spirituality of the Church," in *Theological Investigations*, vol. 20: *Concern for the Church*, trans. Edward Quinn (New York: Crossroad, 1981), 149.

30. Therese of Lisieux, "PN 5, My Song for Today," in *The Poetry of Saint Therese of Lisieux: Complete Edition*, trans. Donald Kinney (Washington, DC: ICS Publications, 1995), 50.

PART TWO:
A THEOLOGY OF
THE SENSES

INTRODUCTION

1. *De Principiis* I, 1, 7.

CHAPTER 1:
TOUCHING WHAT ESCAPES US

1. Juhani Pallasmaa, *The Eyes of the Skin: Architecture and the Senses* (Chichester: John Wiley, 2005), 10.

2. Sophia de Mello Breyner Andresen, *Os três reis do Oriente* (Three Kings from the East) (Lisbon: Estúdios Cor, 1965).

3. Jean-Luc Nancy, *Noli Me Tangere: On the Raising of the Body*, trans. Sarah Clift, Pascale-Anne Brault, and Michael Naas (New York: Fordham University Press, 2008), 37.

4. Augustine, *Confessions*, trans. Carolyn J.-B. Hammond (Cambridge: Harvard University Press, 2014), 10:6, p. 81.

5. Henri Focilon, *In Praise of Hands*, trans. Victoria Charles (New York: Parkstone Press, 2016; orig. Fr. ed. 1934).

6. Tonino Guerra, "La Farfalla." Available at http://museo toninoguerra.com/it/poesie/la-farfalla/.

7. Meister Eckhart, "Sermon 24," in *Meister Eckhart: Teacher and Preacher*, ed. Bernard McGinn (New York: Paulist Press, 1986), 286.

CHAPTER 2:
YEARNING FOR
INFINITE FLAVOR

1. Cynicism was an ascetic philosophical movement founded by Antisthenes of Athens in the fourth century BC.

2. *Bava Batra*, 12b.

3. Henry David Thoreau, *Walden* (Boston: Houghton, Mifflin, 1897), 129.

4. Milan Kundera, *Slowness*, trans. Linda Asher (New York: Harper Collins, 1996), 39.

5. Antoine de Saint-Exupéry, *The Little Prince*, trans. Katherine Woods (San Diego: Harcourt Brace Jovanovich, 1943), 89–90.

6. Ignatius of Loyola, *The Spiritual Exercises*, in *Ignatius of Loyola: The Spiritual Exercises and Selected Works*, trans. George E. Ganss (Mahwah, NJ: Paulist Press, 1991), 121.

7. Tonino Guerra, "L'aria." Available at http://museotonino guerra.com/it/poesie/l-aria/.

8. Simone Weil, *Gravity and Grace*, trans. Emma Crawford and Mario von der Ruhr (London: Routledge, 1952), 117.

9. Oscar Wilde, *Lady Windermere's Fan*, in *The Importance of Being Earnest and Other Plays* (New York: Pocket Books, 2005), 161.

10. Angelus Silesius, "Without Why," trans. Mihai Spariosu, in *Dionysus Reborn: Play and the Aesthetic Dimension in Modern Philosophical and Scientific Discourse* (Ithaca: Cornell University Press, 1989), 118.

11. António Ramos Rosa, *Voz inicial* (Lisbon: Morais, 1960).

CHAPTER 3:
THE SCENT OF THE
PRESENT MOMENT

1. [Translator's note: The Hebrew word *peh*, translated here, in the NRSV, as the "collar" of his robes—suggesting to modern readers the fringe around the neck of the garment—literally means "edge" and is translated in many translations to mean the garment's bottom edge or hem, at the ankles.]

2. Michel de Montaigne, "Of Smells," in *Essays*, trans. Charles Cotton (New York: Charles Scribner, 1902), I, LV.

3. Edward T. Hall, *The Hidden Dimension* (Garden City, NY: Doubleday, 1966), 43.

4. Fernando Pessoa, *The Book of Disquiet*, trans. Alfred MacAdam (New York: Pantheon Books, 1991), 110.

5. Marcel Proust, *Swann's Way*, trans. Lydia Davis (New York: Viking, 2002), 47.

6. Ludwig Wittgenstein, *Philosophical Investigations*, trans. G. E. M. Anscombe (Oxford: Blackwell, 2001), 610.

7. G. K. Chesterton, *Orthodoxy* (New York: Doubleday, 1908), 121.

8. See *Summa Theologica* IIa IIae, q. 136, art. 4.

9. Giacomo Leopardi, *Zibaldone*, trans. Michael Caesar et al. (New York: Farrar, Straus and Giroux, 2013), 100.

CHAPTER 4:
LISTEN TO THE MELODY
OF THE PRESENT MOMENT

1. Timothy Fry, ed., *The Rule of St. Benedict in English* (Collegeville, MN: Liturgical Press, 1981), 15.

2. Francisco de Quevedo, "Amor Constante Mas Allá de la Muerte" [Love Constant Beyond Death], trans. A. Z. Foreman, *Poems Found in Translation* (blog), accessed November 25, 2020, http://poemsintranslation.blogspot.com/2012/10/quevedo-love -constant-beyond-death-from.html.

3. Evagrius Ponticus, *Chapters on Prayer*, no. 11.

4. Rabindranath Tagore, *The Gardener* (New York: Macmillan, 1915), 14–15.

5. Franz Kafka, *Letters to Felice*, trans. James Stern and Elisabeth Duckworth (New York: Schocken, 2016), 156.

6. *The Sayings of The Desert Fathers*, trans. Benedicta Ward (Kalamazoo, MI: Cistercian, 1984), 13.

7. Helen Wadell, ed., *The Desert Fathers* (Ann Arbor: University of Michigan Press, 1957), 63 (corrected for some archaism).

8. Pope Benedict XVI, General Audience, August 31, 2011, http://w2.vatican.va/content/benedict-xvi/en/audiences/2011/ documents/hf_ben-xvi_aud_20110831.html.

CHAPTER 5:
LOOKING THROUGH THE OPEN
DOOR OF THE PRESENT MOMENT

1. Fernando Pessoa, "The Startling Reality of Things," in *Poems of Fernando Pessoa*, trans. Edwin Honig and Susan M. Brown (San Francisco: City Lights, 1986), 28.

2. Simone Weil, "Factory Journal," in *Formative Writings: 1929–1941*, trans. Dorothy Tuck McFarland and Wilhelmina Van Ness (New York: Routledge, 1987), 123.

3. Isak Dinesen, *Out of Africa* (New York: Modern Library, 1937), 238.

4. Antonio Vieira, *Sermões*, 16 vols. (Lisbon, 1959), V: 98.

5. Roland Barthes, *Fragments d'un discours amoureux* (Paris: Éditions du Seuil, 1977), 628.

6. Paraphrase of the words of a character in Marcel Proust, *Remembrance of Things Past*, vol. 5: *The Prisoner*, trans. C. K. Moncrief (London: Chatto & Windus, 1929).

7. Rosa Luxemburg, *Letters from Prison*, trans. Eden and Cedar Paul (Berlin: Young International, 1923), 55.

8. Luxemburg, *Letters*, 55.

9. Luxemburg, *Letters*, 57.

10. Luxemburg, *Letters*, 58.

11. Luxemburg, *Letters*, 58.

12. Simone Weil, "Reflections on the Right Use of School Studies with a View to the Love of God," in *Waiting on God*, trans. Emma Crauford (New York: Fontana Books, 1959), 67.

13. See Maurice Merleau-Ponty, *Phenomenology of Perception*, trans. Donald A. Landes (New York: Routledge, 2012).

14. Matsuo Basho, "The Narrow Wood to the Deep North," in *The Narrow Wood to the Deep North and Other Travel Sketches*, trans. Nobuyuki Yuasa (New York: Penguin, 1966), 97.

CONCLUSION

1. *Finding Our Tongues: Mothers, Infants and the Origin of Language* (New York: Basic Books, 2009).